Paul Davis was educated at Ysgol Gyfun Rhydfelen and then the Dyfed College of Art. He worked as an illustrator and researcher for the Dyfed Archaeological Trust and the Dyfed County Council. He is now a surveyor in Cardiff. His other publications include *Castles of Glamorgan, Castles of Dyfed, Castles of the Welsh Princes, Historic West Wales, Lost Churches of Wales and the Marches* (with Susan Lloyd-Fern) and *Historic Inns and Taverns of Wales and the Marches.*

HISTORIC GOWER

Paul R. Davis

CHRISTOPHER DAVIES

To G.J. and J.O. –
The Red Headed League
and the Spanish Inquisition

Published in 1997 by
Christopher Davies (Publishers) Ltd.
P.O. Box 403, Swansea, SA1 4YF

A CIP catalogue record for this book is
available from the British Library.

ISBN 0 7154 0732 5

Printed and bound in Wales by
Dinefwr Press
Rawlings Road, Llandybie
Carmarthenshire, SA18 3YD

All the illustrations and photographs belong to the author with the exception of the aerial views on pages 75 and 92 – Copyright reserved: National Monuments Record for Wales RCAHM, Plas Crug, Aberystwyth.

Cover photographs:
Front cover – Pennard Castle (main picture) *Mike Collier Photography, Swansea;* Penrice Castle Gatehouse and Arthur's Stone, Reynoldston *Paul R. Davis.*
Back cover – Ilston Church, Swansea Castle, Penrice Church, Oystermouth Castle and Llangennith Church *Paul R. Davis.*

CONTENTS

INTRODUCTION

'Llanddewi, a parish church so named as in the Welsh tongue it signifieth the church of St. David's ... within the lordship of Llanddewi was an old castle of that name'.

Rice Merrick c.1578.

'The Common people call it Arthur's Stone, by a lift of vulgar imagination attributing to that Hero an extravagant size and strength'.

John Williams of Swansea 1693.

'Oystermouth castle is a majestic ruin, in a bold situation near the sea coast, commanding a delightful prospect of the country, and surrounded by broken cliffs'.

Benjamin Malkin c.1803.

For centuries the rich archeological heritage of Gower has drawn travellers and historians to this land, eager to explore, and in some cases exploit, the diversity of monuments and relics left here by ancient Man. The peninsula of Gower is an undulating arm of limestone stretching for over 20km into the Bristol Channel, between the estuaries of the Tawe and Loughor rivers. The southern side is indented with numerous little bays and rocky headlands ceaselessly pounded by the waves; in contrast the north coast is an untroubled expanse of dunes, heaths and bird haunted marshlands. At the eastern edge spreads the modern city of Swansea, while at the furthest point of the peninsula the scattered farms and cottages grow fewer, until the bare land tumbles into the waters of Carmarthen Bay.

For such a relatively small area of land Gower contains an astonishing variety of sites and monuments reflecting every phase of Man's existence in Britain for the last 70 millennia or more. The most outstanding structures such as churches, castles and megalithic monuments have long been known to antiquarians, but since the last century the pioneering work of archaeologists, local historians and field researchers has greatly increased the number of known sites, from the obvious to the inconspicuous. many modern visitors to Gower will be aware of this historic legacy; but some, exploring the more prominent and better displayed monuments, will pass many others by, simply because the travellers may not be aware of their existence, or recognise them for what they are.

The Age of Stone

A chipped stone tool discovered near Rhossili in 1978 is the earliest piece of evidence to indicate the presence of Man in Gower. The primitive implement is a hand held axe archaeologists believe was made some time in the *Lower Palaeolithic* period over 75000 years ago. The *Palaeolithic* or Old Stone Age lasted from about c.250,000 BC to 8000 BC, a vast period of time which encompassed many changes in climate and topography, when the land mass later to be known as Britain was periodically buried under extensions of the north polar ice cap. The retreat and return of the ice affected sea levels, and all along the south and west coasts of Gower can be seen masses of stone and gravel cemented together by blown sand, known as breccia or 'raised beaches', which mark the levels of the old coastlines. Evidence from the excavations and ransackings of early archaeologists on deposits safely buried in caves has revealed the bones of animals that roamed the land all those millennia ago; rhino, hippo, straight-tusked elephant and lion were here during the warmer interglacial periods, while mammoth, wholly rhino, reindeer and cave bear were adapted for life during the colder times.

Early Man depended on these animals for food and clothing and small tribes of hunters roamed the land in search of game, unhindered by the seas that now separate Britain from the rest of Europe. Evidence for human activity in this remote period is extremely scanty, and depends solely on the chance discovery of characteristic stone and flint implements. A worked bone tool discovered in Longhole cave (39) may be of *Middle Palaeolithic* date c.50,000-36,000 BC but colonisation began in earnest in the *Upper Palaeolithic* after c.36000 BC. Over five thousand stone implements have been recovered from Goat's Hole Cave, Paviland (40), which is reckoned to be one of the richest Upper Palaeolithic sites in Britain; yet in all probability there were only a few hundred people living in Britain at this time, hunting for food on the great plains that stretched before the Gower escarpment, and using caves and rock shelters as temporary campsites before moving on. The vacated caves would then be used as dens by wolves and hyenas, leaving the remains of their prey for future archaeologists to find.

From around 25000 BC the climate deteriorated and the ice slowly crept over the land, rendering Britain uninhabitable. The warming climate after c.10,000 BC encouraged more people to spread northwards once more into Britain, living as their predecessors had done, by fishing, hunting and foraging in the newly afforested lands. The whereabouts of these 'hunter-gatherers' can be detected by the discovery of flint tools and the waste from their manufacture. Since the 1960's ploughing of the uplands has churned up thousands of flints, and distinctive 'microlithic' tools of the *Mesolithic* period (c.8,000-4,000 BC) have also been found at Burry Holms (53), Cathole (17) and Mewslade caves (47). There was a dramatic change in the landscape as the ice caps melted causing a rise in sea level and the loss of extensive coastal lands in relatively short space of geological time. Britain

Goat's Hole cave, Paviland.

became an island in the seventh millennium BC, and the great plain in front of the Gower escarpment was slowly eaten into by the sea, a process which eventually formed the sea cliffs along the south coast.

During the *Neolithic* or New Stone Age (c.4,000-c.2,500 BC) Man first began to domesticate animals and develop a basic agricultural system, so that in time the vagaries and dangers of the hunt were replaced by a more stable society. Unlike the earlier Ages of Man, stone tools are not the only relics of this period, for these first farmers were builders as well, and the structures they raised five thousand years ago still survive today. Simple huts and dwelling sites have been excavated elsewhere in Wales, and traces of a settlement were found under a later burial mound on Cefn Bryn, but the most tangible Neolithic monuments are the stone tombs constructed to house the remains of the dead. These tombs are known in Welsh as a *cromlech* and consist of a stone chamber formed of upright slabs and roofed over with a large capstone. The chamber was enclosed within a mound of stones (a *cairn*) or earth (a *barrow*), usually of oblong plan, with the tomb located at one end. Two sites in Gower, at Park Cwm (16) and Penmaen Burrows (20), belong to a distinctive type of Neolithic tomb found mainly in the area of the Severn Valley and Cotswold Hills. These have smaller burial compartments branching off a central passageway approached along a funnel shaped *forecourt*, where rituals and ceremonies were no doubt carried out. It is thought that Neolithic burial practices were similar to those of North American Indians, in that the body was allowed to decay naturally and only the bones were placed in the tomb. These repositories were designed for continual use, and the entrance would be sealed after each inhumation. Despite the massive materials used in their construction few tombs survive in their original state, and the stony cairns have usually been despoiled, leaving the chambers standing stark and bare.

The Age of Metal

At the beginning of the second millennium BC a further influx of continental immigrants brought with them implements of bronze, and introduced the knowledge of basic metal working, heralding the *Bronze Age* (c.2,000-500 BC). With better tools man began to shape the landscape with greater success than the older primitive stone implements allowed. A few dwelling sites have been found but as with the Neolithic period it is the monuments associated with rituals and death that are the most plentiful and enduring relics of this age. Yet there is one very important difference between the burial practices, in that the Bronze Age cairns were raised over individual graves. Secondary or multiple burials are not unknown, but the majority of cairns mark the resting place of just one person, pointing to a developing hierarchial social structure. There are well over 400 cairns in Glamorgan alone, more than in any other Welsh county, and yet this figure can hardly reflect the number of people who lived and died in a space of some two thousand years; in all likelihood only the aristocracy and important members of society were interred in this fashion. Bodies were generally cremated and the remains placed in an earthenware urn within a stone 'coffin' or cist dug into the ground. Very often prized possessions such as flint or bronze knives would be placed in the grave, as well as tiny 'pigmy cups' containing food offerings for the after-life. When Carn Goch (71) was dug up in 1855 nine urns including two pigmy cups were found, most probably representing secondary burials inserted into the mound over

An exposed burial cist on Mynydd Drumau.

several generations. Once the capstone was in place the cist was covered with a round heap of earth or stones.

By the present day the damage caused by natural weathering, stone robbing and amateur archaeologists has affected Bronze Age cairns to the extent that few remain in the form they were originally built. Often the covering mound has been removed leaving the cist exposed, as can be seen at Llanmadoc Hill (61). Excavations on several Gower cairns has revealed how complex these innocuous looking mounds can be. Just before Pennard Birch round cairn was destroyed in 1941 to make way for the Swansea airport it was thoroughly excavated and a typical burial cist was revealed. The presence of charcoal indicated that a ritual pyre of oak branches had been burned over the cist and the grave was then covered with a mound of stones. This was then encircled with a stone ring 6.1m across, and then buried under a turf and clay mound. A second ring was constructed around the site and then the entire monument was covered with a domed mound of clay up to 1.8m high and 22.9m across. Another destroyed site at Colt's Hill, Oystermouth, was also revealed to be a complex multi-layered mound which had been raised over an earlier dwelling hut.

Despite the wear and tear of the centuries, several types of burial mound have been identified, and the most common is the *round cairn*, which has a profile like an overturned bowl. Rarer *platform cairns* are flat disc-like mounds, often with an encircling kerb of stones to help retain the structure. *Ring cairns* are circular or oval enclosures which mainly appear to be ritual

An excavated and partially reconstructed ring cairn on Cefn Bryn.

or ceremonial monuments rather than sepulchral. Some cairns have elaborate kerbs or stone settings such as the splendid Carn Llechart (72), where a ring of 25 upright slabs enclose a central cist.

Standing stones and stone circles were also erected during the Bronze Age as part of the ceremonies that formed such an important part of tribal life. There are no circles in Gower, but a striking number of standing stones have been recorded by the Royal Commission on Ancient and Historical Monuments. Eleven are considered to be genuine Prehistoric monuments, but that number increases to over thirty if field name evidence, documented lost sites and possible cattle rubbing stones are included. No-one knows for certain why these stones were set up, and archeological investigations have pointed to no single function. Some were gravestones, others may have been boundary markers or shrines, but excavations on sites outside Gower have revealed that the stone is very often the only visible remnant of a much larger ritual complex; cobbled surfaces, ritual burials, timber structures, and even hundreds of tiny upright stones have been found.

The predominance of sepulchral and ceremonial monuments which characterises the Bronze Age gave way in the first century BC to the appearance of hillforts and defended settlements. During the *Iron Age* (c.500 BC-c.100 AD), as bronze was replaced by a more durable metal, hundreds of fortifications were built in response to the highly developed, and perhaps aggressive, society of the late Bronze Age. Another factor which may have contributed to the proliferation of defended settlements was the loss of agricultural land due to a climatic deterioration. During the first millennium BC the climate was much wetter than it is today, upland forests decayed forming peat bogs, rendering high ground unsuitable for settlements and causing a shift in population to better drained lands. These forts may well have been built on hilltops for dryness as much as defence.

There are over thirty sites in Gower which are likely to belong to the Iron Age, or were constructed by native groups during the Roman period. Of

Mynydd Drumau: Carreg Bica standing stone.

these only one, Cilifor (69), can be classed as a true hillfort, where the defences are quite substantial and enclose an area of almost 3 hectares. The remainder are much smaller defended homesteads or farmsteads, with only Hardings Down west fort (56) and The Bulwark (61) displaying extensive fortifications. No modern excavations have taken place on the large Gower forts, but several of the smaller sites have been comprehensively investigated since the last war. From one of three dwelling huts at Hardings Down came potsherds dating to c.100-50 BC, while at The Knave (44) only two

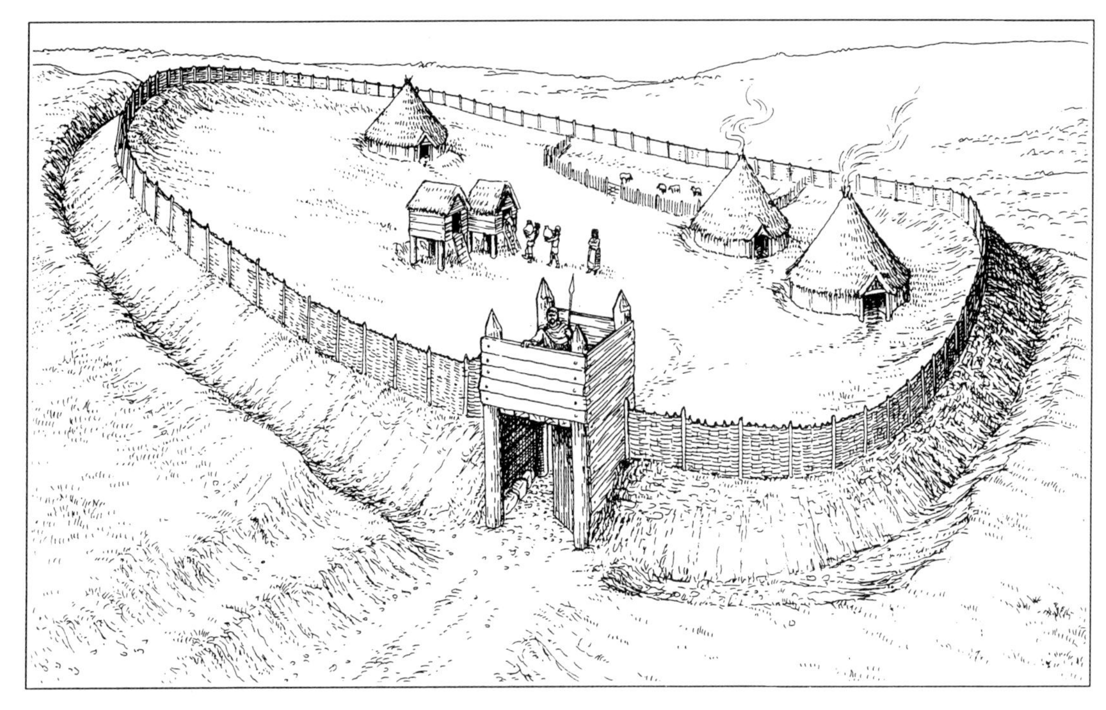

A conjectural reconstruction of Hardings Down West Fort in the 1st century BC.

huts were located along with pottery fragments of c.50 BC-50 AD. High Pennard (12) produced finds of the late 1st-2nd century AD, and the site of three round huts; a similar age was suggested by finds from the Bishopston Valley fort (13), though only one hut was found. At a small enclosure on Kilvey Hill (76) a 2nd century AD potsherd was found beneath the rampart, proving that the defences had been built well after the Roman invasion.

These huts usually survive today as faint circular depressions on the ground, and so without full-scale excavation of the interior, some could be missed by just a surface examination. Nevertheless, the piecemeal evidence from Gower sites suggests that most settlements sheltered only one or two farming families at most. The defences invariably consisted of rubble or earth banks fronted with ditches. There is evidence that some ramparts were reinforced with drystone walling, and there would have been additional protection in the form of a wooden fence, a stockade, or a viciously practical thorn hedge along the crest of the bank. Wherever possible, the forts relied on natural defences such as steep hillsides and sloping ground, and the sheer cliffs of the coastline enabled the builders of promontory forts like Horse Cliff (42) and Old Castle (49), to worry about massing the defences on the vulnerable landward flank alone.

The Roman Period and Dark Ages

A Celtic tribe known as the Silures ruled south-east Wales at the time of the Roman invasion, and offered support and shelter to the Belgic leader

Comparative plans of Iron Age hillforts (open circles denote hut sites).

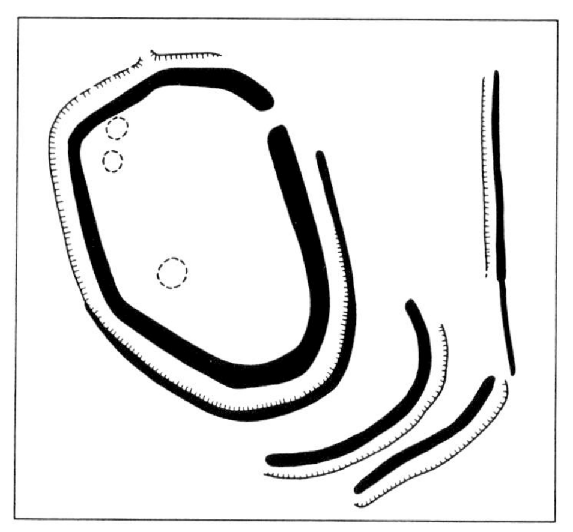

Hardings Down West Fort.

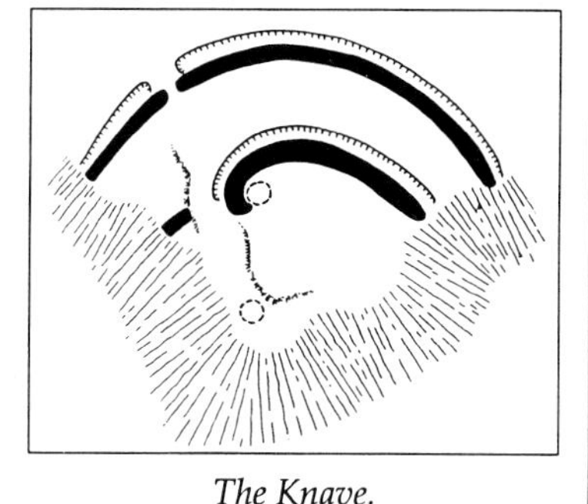

The Knave.

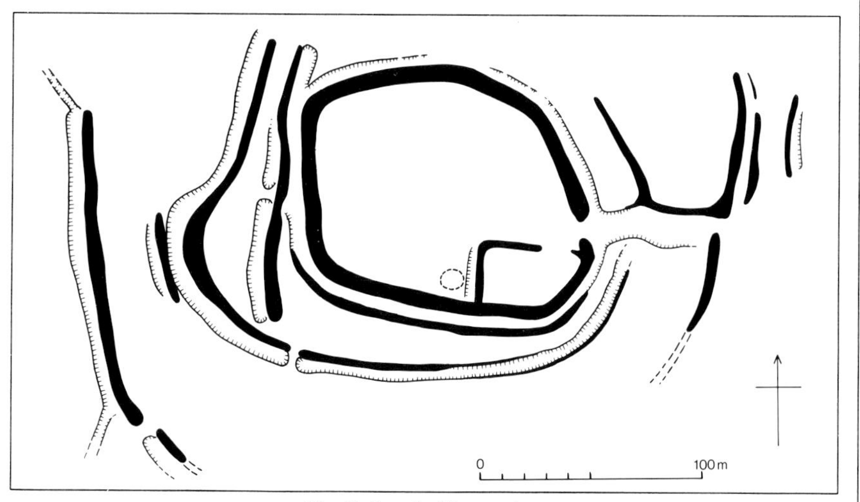

The Bulwark, Llanmadoc.

Caratacus in his struggle against the invaders. By the 7th decade of the 1st century AD the tribes had been subdued, and the Romans built a string of forts and military stations around the mountainous heart of south Wales. It was the imperial policy to foster the civilized Roman way of life among native inhabitants of a conquered country, and there is evidence that many tribes were happy enough to accept new lifestyles and consumer goods. Native villas and farmsteads are known to have existed in many parts of lowland Wales, and there was some kind of Roman building at Oystermouth (1), but in Gower the evidence from excavations is that the locals were left very much alone and continued residing in hillforts and cave dwellings. Their Romanised lifestyles continued for many years after the troops were officially withdrawn from Britain in AD 410, pottery was still imported from the Mediterranean, and Latin inscriptions carved on burial stones during the 5th and early 6th centuries.

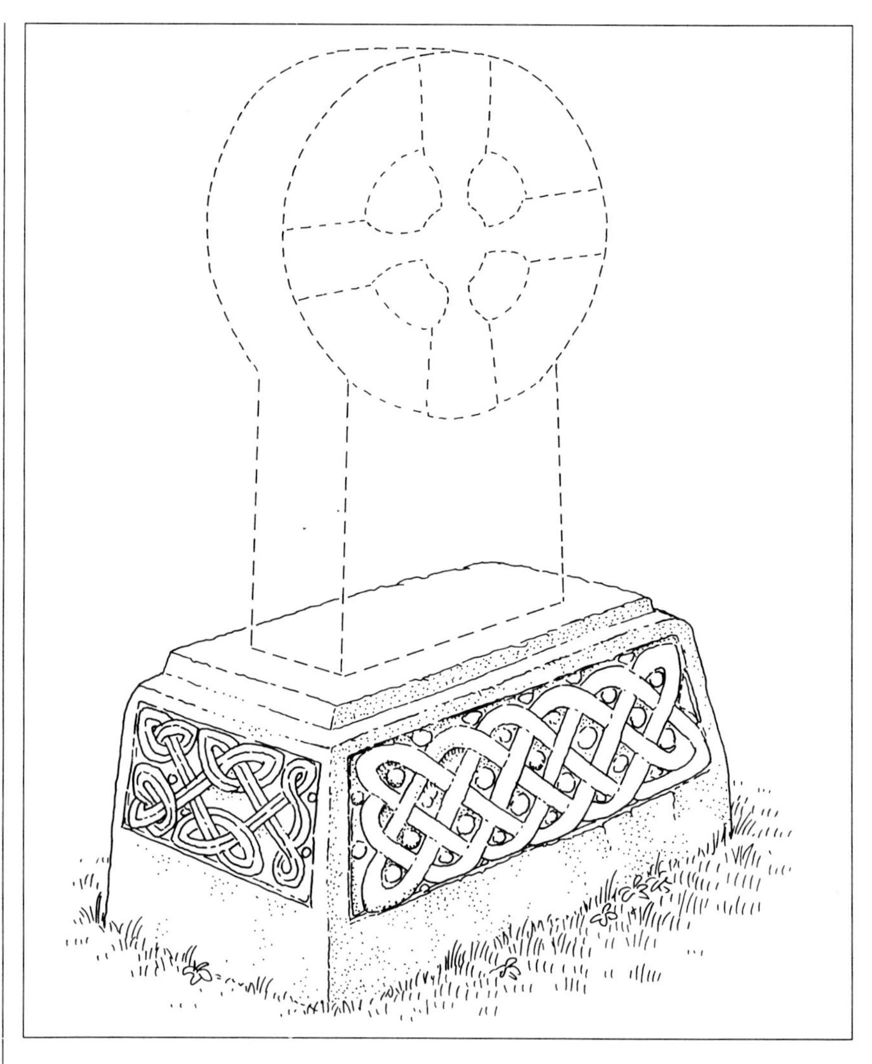

A reconstruction of the Llangyfelach wheel-cross. The cross head would no doubt have been as richly decorated as the base.

The great engineering feats of the Roman period crumbled into ruin with the advent of the *Dark Ages* (5th-11th century AD), a period of strife and warfare, of destruction and legendary endeavour, and against this turbulent backdrop the Christian faith was rapidly spreading through the land. Native saints and holy men such as Dewi, Teilo, Illtyd, Cenydd and their dedicated followers established monastic settlements and small sacred precincts, the precursors of later Medieval churches, which can be identified today by place-name evidence, Celtic gravestones, and circular churchyards, eg. Llangyfelach (79). Virtually nothing survives above ground of the Dark Age church in Gower, although foundations of earlier structures beneath Medieval buildings have been detected at Burry Holms (53) and Llanelen (70). The monuments of this period take the form of grave markers and sculptured stones, and the earliest ones have Latin inscriptions, such as the Vectus stone at Llanmadoc (60); The person commemorated was prob-

Llanmadoc Church: two Dark Age cross stones have been set into the wall of the nave.

ably an important member of the local community or one of the ruling classes. From the 6th century onwards inscribed slabs were superseded by plainer headstones carved with a cross, which in turn developed into more elaborate and highly distinctive examples of Celtic art, such as 'St Cenydd's gravestone' at Llangennith (55) and the leper stone, Llanrhidian (67).

During the Early Middle Ages Wales was divided into several small kingdoms and territories ruled by individual princes, almost continuously at war with each other. A ruthless and charismatic figure might force some semblance of order on this turbulent society, but the results were always short-lived. From the 8th century onwards the land was plagued by Viking attacks; Llangennith was sacked by the Norsemen and there is a tradition that a settlement or trading post was established where Swansea now stands.

The Middle Ages

The greatest cultural and topographical change to the peninsula occurred in the early years of the 12th century with the arrival of the Normans, themselves of Viking descent. The conquest of lowland England was achieved fairly quickly after 1066, but attempts to bring Wales under the sway of the English crown were to take a further two centuries, and even then the pacification was not entirely successful. The invasion of south Wales began in 1093 and an attempt to seize Gower may have taken place by 1100, but within a few years King Henry I had entrusted control of the territory to his Welsh ally, Hywel ap Goronwy. Hywel's murder in 1106 gave the King the opportunity to claim Gower as Norman land, and he granted the prize to Henry de Beaumont, Earl of Warwick (d.1119). Earl Henry and his successors embarked on a policy of military subjugation and colonisation, establishing a main stronghold and administrative centre at Swansea, and parcelling out the land among chosen followers. Gower became a marcher lordship and its ruler was in effect a king within his own territory.

The early lordship included a very large upland area between the Tawe and Loughor rivers extending as far north as Glanamman, and for most of the Medieval period this tract was left under nominal Welsh control. Thus grew two distinct areas, the Norman-held peninsula and rich agricultural lands *Gower Anglicana*, and the less hospitable uplands *Gower Wallicana*. This division remained despite sporadic raids by the Welsh, and was an important factor in the development of Gower culture and society; the plethora of English place-names in south Gower is evidence of this.

The knights and followers of the lords of Gower were granted chunks of land within the more securely held part of the peninsula. They built castles to provide a military foothold, and then encouraged the growth of villages to bring some measure of economic stability. Lands were also granted to churches and monastic houses. The Norman take-over was not a purely one-sided affair, and the chronicles of the period record many attempts by the Welsh to reclaim their lands, the most serious took place in 1215-1217 when the princes of Dyfed, aided by Llywelyn Fawr of Gwynedd, succeeded in temporarily ending Norman rule. After the last Earl of Warwick died childless in 1184 Gower was held by the Crown, until King John granted the lordship to the powerful De Breose family in 1203, with whom it remained for over a century. In the second half of the 13th century the princely house of Gwynedd under Llywelyn ap Gruffudd again succeeded in uniting the Welsh rulers, bringing warfare to the south, and Swansea was attacked in 1257. Thirty years later, Rhys ap Maredudd of Dyfed launched another attack on the town.

By the end of the 13th century the Welsh rulers had been effectively crushed, and the land of Gower could have expected a long period of peace, but there was further trouble during the misgoverned reign of Edward II and, more seriously, at the beginning of the 15th century when the dispirited Welsh populace rose in revolt under the charismatic leadership of Owain Glyndŵr. During the 14th, 15th and 16th centuries the lordship was held by succession of noble families, the Mowbrays, Beauchamps, and Herberts, though they had large estates elswhere and were in effect absentee landlords, having little effect on the area.

A great architectural change occurred during the Middle Ages as castles, churches and houses sprung up through the landscape, dominating all that had been built before except, perhaps, the huge earthworks of the Iron Age. Castles are the most familiar relic of this period and epitomise the ruthless ambitions of the ruling Normans. The earliest castle types were crude and simple structures relying on earthwork and timber defences, which could be built in a relatively short time – a very necessary factor when invading a potentially hostile territory. The most widespread fortification was the *motte and bailey*, consisting of a heavily defended timber tower, or keep, set on top of a conical mound (the 'motte'). An adjoining courtyard enclosure (the 'bailey') contained ancillary buildings such as stores, stables, workshops and barracks. Curiously, in Gower there is only one surviving motte and bailey, at Talybont (77), and all the other early castles are *ringworks*, which consist of a roughly circular enclosure surrounded with a strong rampart and ditch. Some are built on natural scarps or promontories like the earlier forts of the Iron Age, with only a single bank and ditch on the weaker landward flank.

In 1898 William Morgan excavated part of Old Barland Camp ringwork near Bishopston and found the post holes of a timber palisade and walkway along the crest of the rampart. More detailed excavations at Castle Tower (21) by Leslie Alcock in 1960, revealed a substantial timber tower astride the bank which doubled as a keep and gatehouse. Foundations of simple halls and buildings have been noted within ringworks at Penmaen, Pennard (9), Norton (27) and Loughor (80). These earth and timber forts may have been cheap and quick to assemble, but they had a limited life and during the 13th century the defences began to be upgraded with masonry walls and towers. In turn, the large stone castles were also left to fall into decay in less war-like days, when fortified houses such as Weobley (65) and Landimore (64) were considered sufficient for the protection of the wealthy aristocracy and their estates.

The Norman invasion also wrought changes to the ecclesiastical establishment in Gower; the old Welsh college or 'bangor' at Llangennith was reformed as a Benedictine priory under the control of a French abbey, and many churches and manors became the property of religious orders such as the Knights Hospitallers. During this period the plain and simple native churches were rebuilt and extended on a larger scale, though none have the grandeur and refinement of the richer English parish churches. What sur-

A cutaway reconstruction of Weobley Castle.

vives of the Medieval buildings today is rarely the product of just one phase of construction; additions, alterations, renovations and rebuilding went on over the centuries so that a single church can display several architectural styles. it would appear that most Gower churches originally comprised a rectangular nave (where the congregation was seated) with a chancel (containing the high altar) adjoining the east end. This simple and basic layout can now be seen at the restored churches of Nicholaston (23) and Reynoldston (31), and the ruined chapels at Penmaen Burrows (19), Burry Holms (53) and Rhossili (48).

In later years, as money was made available, additions to the building were carried out; a transept or side chapel was often built out from the nave, as at Penrice (29) and Llandeilo Talybont (77). Towers were increasingly popular in the later Middle Ages and in Gower they take two forms: the familiar battlemented type very much like a castle tower, eg. Oystermouth (1) and Bishopston (6); and those with 'saddleback' or gabled roofs, as at Llanddewi (36) and Llanmadoc (60). The tower was usually positioned at the west end of the nave creating an almost archetypal church plan, but at Ilston (15) and Llangennith (55) the towers are on the side wall, and at Cheriton (62) it occupies a central position between the chancel and nave.

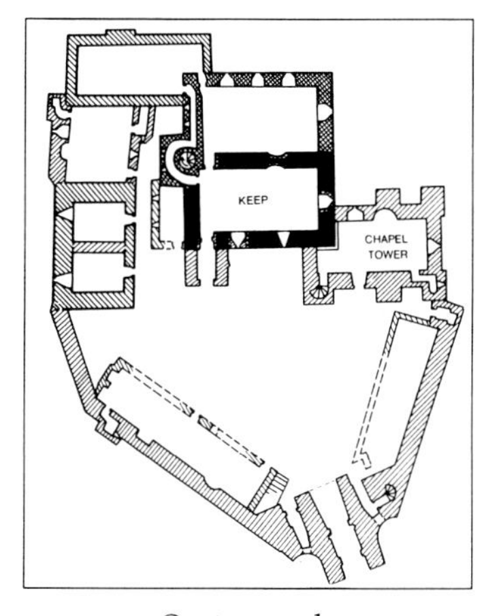

Oystermouth.

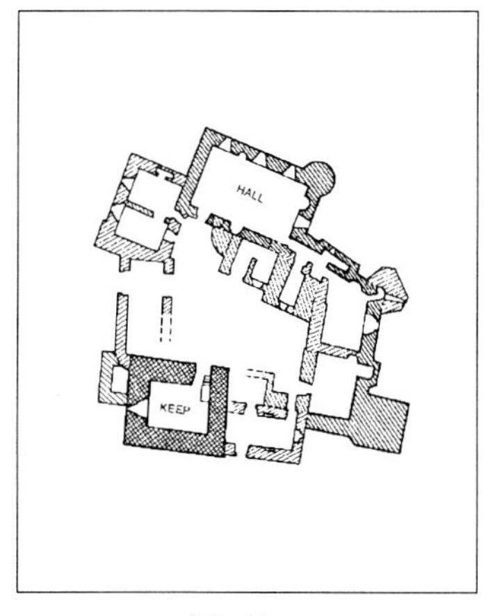

Weobley.

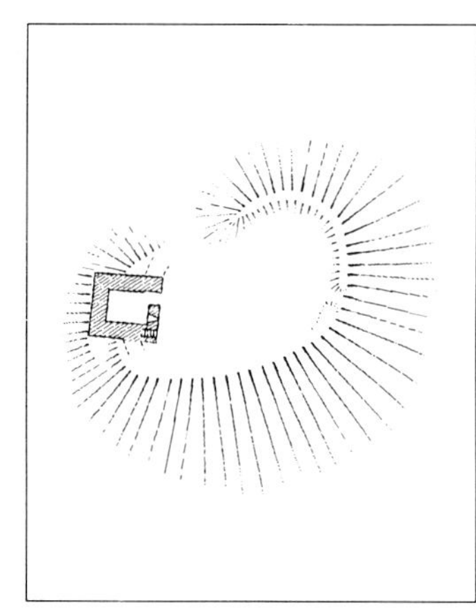

Loughor.

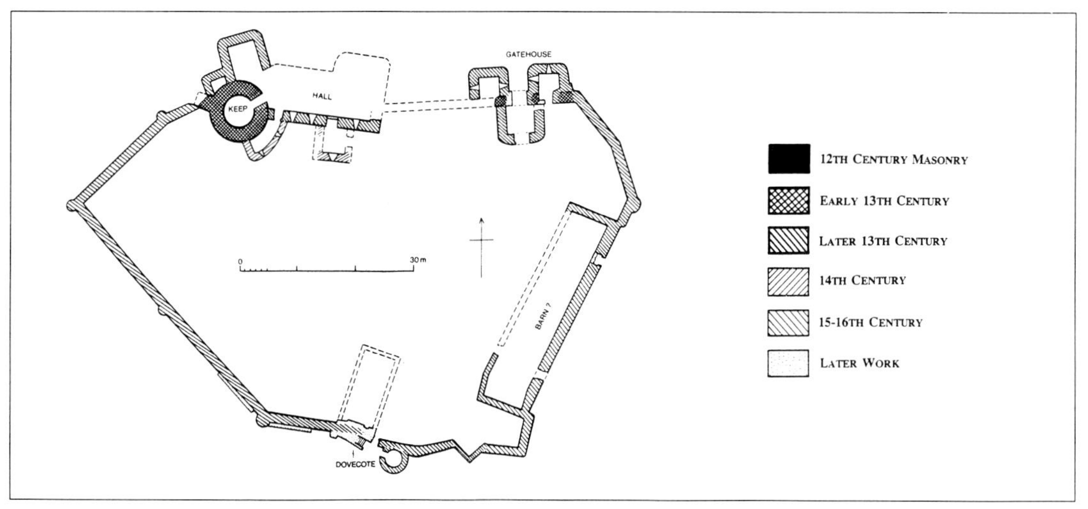

Penrice.

Comparative plans of some Gower castles.

The impression a visitor gets of church interiors today is one of stark purity, with bare whitewashed walls and no ostentatious displays except, perhaps, at the altar; but Medieval churches were very different. The tomb effigies at Oxwich (24) and Llangennith were probably brightly painted, and the walls would have been covered with inscriptions and biblical scenes (which in the case of Llandeilo Talybont were fortunately rediscovered under layers of whitewash and restored). These images were so

Ilston Church.

often done away with at the Reformation and Commonwealth period, and a particular target of the iconoclasts was a *rood loft*, a wooden gallery supporting a large crucifix above the chancel arch. There are no rood images in Gower today (though there is a good modern example in Oxwich church) but their former presence can be detected by supporting brackets or high-level doorways and blocked stair passages. Even the well-meaning hand of the Victorian restorer has considerably altered the overall appearance of many Welsh country churches.

The care and expense lavished on Medieval castles and churches were rarely repeated on the houses of the less well-off. Excavations at the deserted settlements of Pennard (9), Rhossili (48) and Burry Holms (53) have revealed the foundations of rectangular buildings with low walls of stone or turf, formerly with pitched roofs covered with thatch, shingles or slate. The main room (sometimes the only one) was known as the *hall*, and was heated by an open hearth set upon the floor. The smoke escaped through a vent in the roof or the unglazed windows. Re-created Medieval buildings at the museum of Welsh Life, St Fagans, and Cosmeston Park in South Glamorgan give a good impression of the relative comforts of home life for a typical Medieval family. The foundations of long abandoned houses can be seen at Walterston (33), Cefn Drum (73) and Mynydd Drumau (81). Those with more money could afford to live in some degree of comfort; the hall-house at Glebe Farm (62) may date from the 14th century and was a building of

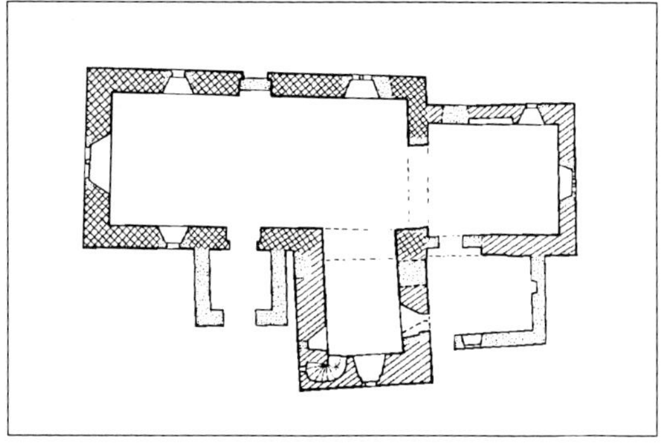

Ilston.

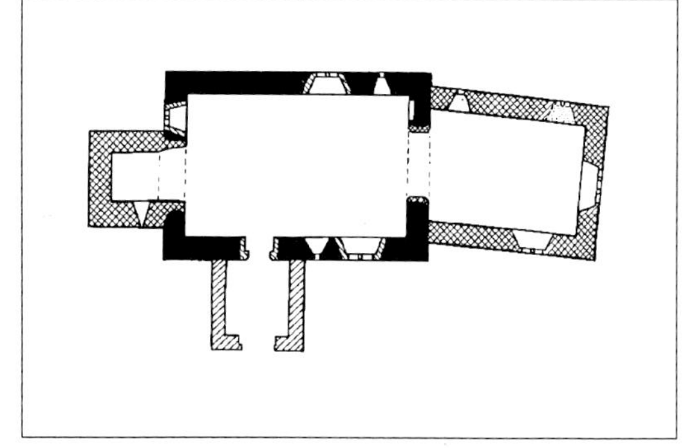

Llanddewi.

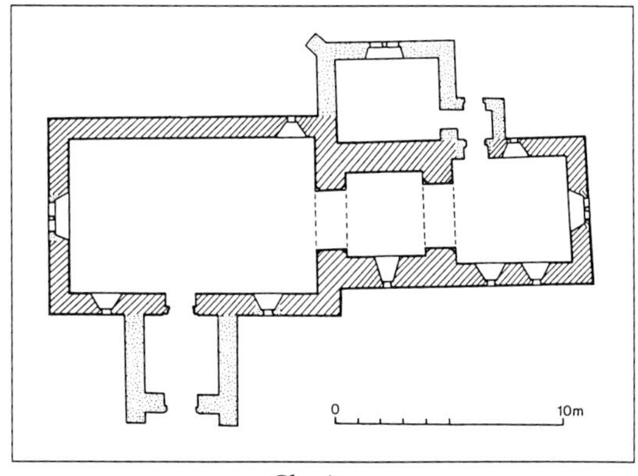

Cheriton.

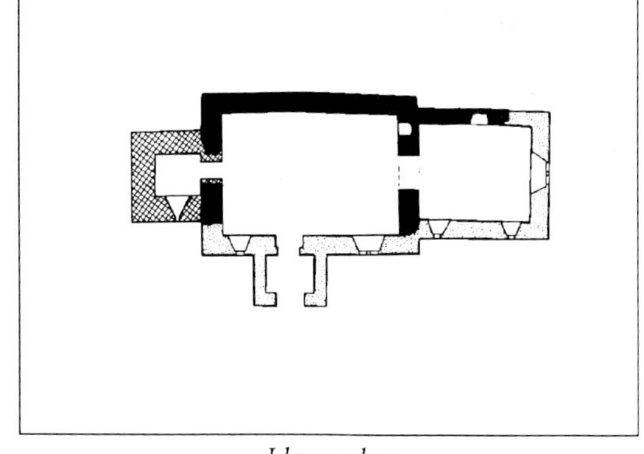

Llanmadoc.

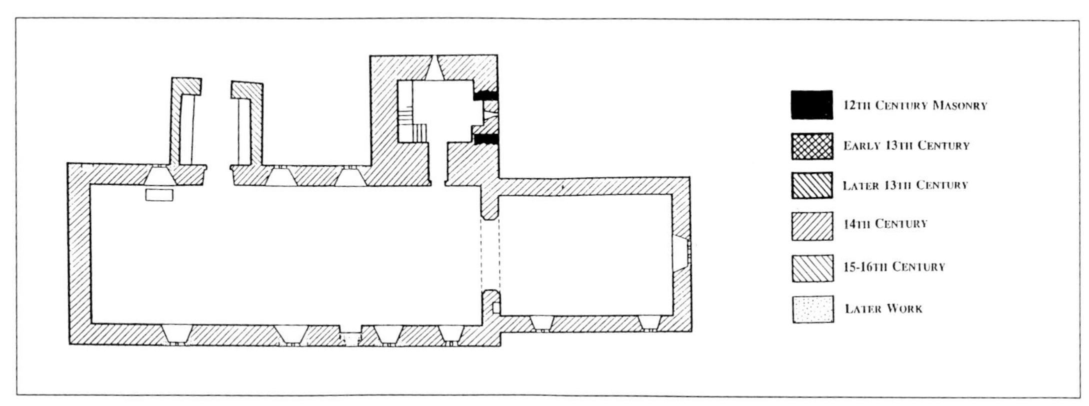

Llangennith.

Comparative plans of some Gower churches.

some importance. The principal room was still a smoky, draughty hall, but the owner's private room, the *solar*, had the luxury of a fireplace!

From the Middle Ages to the Industrial Revolution

During the 16th century a more settled society developed under the stable central government of the Tudors, and the most obvious benefit of the improving economy was the appearance of new houses in parts of Wales. The dark, smoggy Medieval halls of timber or stone construction made way for more durable buildings with enclosed fireplaces and chimneys, and with rooms on more than one floor. A few examples of 16th and early 17th century storied houses survive in Gower, but many have been destroyed in quite recent times; Nottage (2), Backingstone (4) and Oxwich Green (26) are recent casualties, but Great Kittle (5) and Pitt (28) are among the survivors. They were the homes not of poor people, but well-to-do farmers or merchants, while Llanddewi (36) and Oxwich 'castles' (25) belonged to much more affluent owners. Indeed Oxwich is not so much a house as a palace, a grandiose an over-the-top status symbol of the ambitious Mansel family.

The rebuilding of Gower houses went on into the 19th century and many ancient looking cottages with whitewashed walls and thatched roofs (though

Cutaway drawing of Kennexstone Farm, c.1800.

only a pitiful few surviving today) may not be as old as they appear. Gower houses share certain architectural features with the West Country, with which there were strong maritime links, in particular the use of a fireplace and chimney positioned in the side wall, rather than the gable, and also a small projecting wing known as an *outshut*, which usually contained a bed. Kennexstone (59) retains features characteristic of the region and has been reconstructed at the museum of Welsh Life, St Fagans.

By the beginning of the 19th century the Industrial Revolution was underway transforming the south Wales valleys and the Llansamlet area, but Gower was little affected since the peninsula lacked any major deposits of valuable minerals and ores. Some mining for lead and silver was carried out at Bishopston and Mumbles, but the nearest to a large-scale industry was the quarrying of stone for lime burning. There are thought to be over 150 abandoned kilns, most are no older than the 19th century, although Medieval limekilns have been discovered at Burry Holms and Weobley castle. Nevertheless, Gower was not without the small industries essential for the growth of any rural community. There were many fulling mills and corn grinding watermills (no less than eight on the 6km long Burry stream), and there was also a windmill on top of Kilvey Hill (76). The early 19th century mill at Parc Cwm has been restored and is open to the public, and the ruins of abandoned buildings can be seen near Penrice and Llanrhidian.

The most impressive industrial relic in the Swansea valley is Scott's Pit (84) near Llansamlet, an early 19th century engine house designed to pump water out of the underground workings. Of far greater historical importance is the 16th century Salt House (37) at Port Eynon, the only surviving one of several known to have existed in the area. The ruined building has long figured in local legends concerning smugglers and secret passages, and though archaeologists have found evidence of a fortified building here, the Salt House was primarily a factory extracting salt from sea water.

The historian in Gower

The archaeology of the Gower peninsula began to interest historians and antiquarians as far back as the 16th century, with the like of John Leland (1506-1562) and Rice Merrick (d.1587). The information they gathered was often very sketchy and relied much on local information coloured by folklore. A more thorough approach was adopted by the geologist and scholar Edward Llwyd (1660-1709), who sent out questionnaires to various correspondants, as well as rehashing earlier works by William Camden and Merrick. His most meticulous informant was Isaac Hamon of Bishopston, who provided a detailed survey of Gower society and antiquities at the close of the 17th century. Hamon's work is still of great value today, particularly in detailing monuments which have not survived the intervening three centuries.

In the 1740's the brothers Samuel and Nathaniel Buck worked their way through England and Wales as freelance illustrators, providing wealthy landowners with meticulously crafted engravings of the monuments in their ownership. All the main castles of Gower were included in their series of Glamorganshire antiquities, and although a certain amount of artistic licence was employed, the etchings still provide a useful record of what these buildings were like at the time. Earlier sketches by Francis Place (1678) and Thomas Dineley (1684) show the appearance of pre-industrial Swansea when the castle was the most dominant building in the town.

As far as archaeology is concerned, until the latter half of the 19th century (and in some cases even into this century) an 'excavation' merely involved digging up the requisite monument with picks and shovels and seeing what artifacts came to light. Such massacres may well have unearthed many finds, but their relationship to the site and the important evidence of stratigraphy was badly recorded, if at all. Interest in the bone caves of Gower started as far back as 1792, when quarrymen discovered extinct animal bones at Crawley Rocks near Nicholaston. Dean Buckland's celebrated excavation at Paviland in 1823 uncovered a partial skeleton of a Palaeolithic man, though at the time it was thought to have been a woman of Iron Age or Roman date. Many finds from the various diggings found their way into the collection of the Royal Institute of South Wales, which opened the first museum in Wales, at Swansea, in 1841. Members of the Institute included Edward Wood, George Grant Francis, and William Llewellyn Morgan, who contributed much to the further understanding of the history of Swansea and the surrounding area. All had military backgrounds and are today more familiarly known by the title 'colonel', which shows how much archaeology was then the preserve of the upper classes. Col. Wood of Stouthall excavated many of the caves and unearthed a huge quantity of animal bones, as well as Palaeolithic finds from North Hill Tor and Deborah's Hole. In 1899 Col. Morgan published 'An antiquarian survey of East Gower', complementing the four volumes of 'A history of West Gower' (1877–1894) compiled by the rector of Llanmadoc and Cheriton, J. D. Davies. Davies was not only an indefatigable collector of local history and folklore, but also a highly skilled craftsman whose woodcarvings still adorn many Gower churches.

The early years of this century witnessed a renewed interest in the bone caves, and re-examination of Paviland by W. J. Sollas in 1912 brought to light a huge number of Palaeolithic artifacts overlooked by Buckland. In the same year there was a flurry of interest in Bacon Hole when what were thought to be Prehistoric wall paintings were discovered. During the Second World War Audrey Williams carried out a series of excavations on a number of cairns and promontory forts and the results of these, and earlier reports, were summarised in J. G. Rutter's 'Prehistoric Gower' (1948). In the same year the recently formed Gower Society published its first annual journal devoted to the history, culture and wildlife of the peninsula, and it is still in print today. The Society has also produced a number of booklets on churches, caves and castles of the area, and has organised an excavation of

Excavations by the Glamorgan-Gwent Archaeological Trust on the Roman fort at Loughor.

an Iron Age fort on Kilvey Hill, under the direction of Bernard Morris. Leslie Alcock's excavation at Castle Tower, Penmaen, in 1960-61 was an important step in understanding Medieval ringworks, and within a few years the Royal Commission on Ancient and Historical Monuments had undertaken work at Burry Holms and Hardings Down as part of ongoing research into compiling an inventory of Glamorgan monuments.

In the mid 1970's the Glamorgan–Gwent Archeological Trust was set up as one of four bodies dealing primarily with the 'rescue' archaeology of sites in Wales threatened with destruction or redevelopment, and in Gower the Trust has carried out work at the Salt House and Roman Loughor. Aside from excavations, the Trust also maintains an extensive archive which continues to grow as more and more ancient sites are rediscovered and recorded for posterity.

This book is an historical tour through the peninsula and the hinterland beyond Swansea, and since the emphasis is on accessibility, all the sites mentioned here are either open to the public, or lie on or near roads and footpaths. Gower has an excellent network of signposted public footpaths, and the Ordnance Survey maps 1126 and 159 are invaluable tools for exploring the highways and byways of the peninsula. The gazetteer section has been written in a geographical order, travelling from Swansea along the south coast Rhossili, then crossing over to the north side. The variable spellings of Gower place-names has long bedevilled writers, and for the purpose of this book I have opted for the spellings shown on current OS maps. For the reader interested in monuments of a particular period there is a classified list of sites at the back of the book, along with grid references for plotting their location on an OS map. Most of the sites are Scheduled Ancient Monuments and are protected by law. It is an offence to injure or deface them. They have survived to us for thousands of years, and with care and respect they may endure a little longer. In 1956 Gower was designated an Area of Outstanding Natural Beauty – it is up to the consideration of every visitor to keep it so.

Part One

THE GOWER PENINSULA

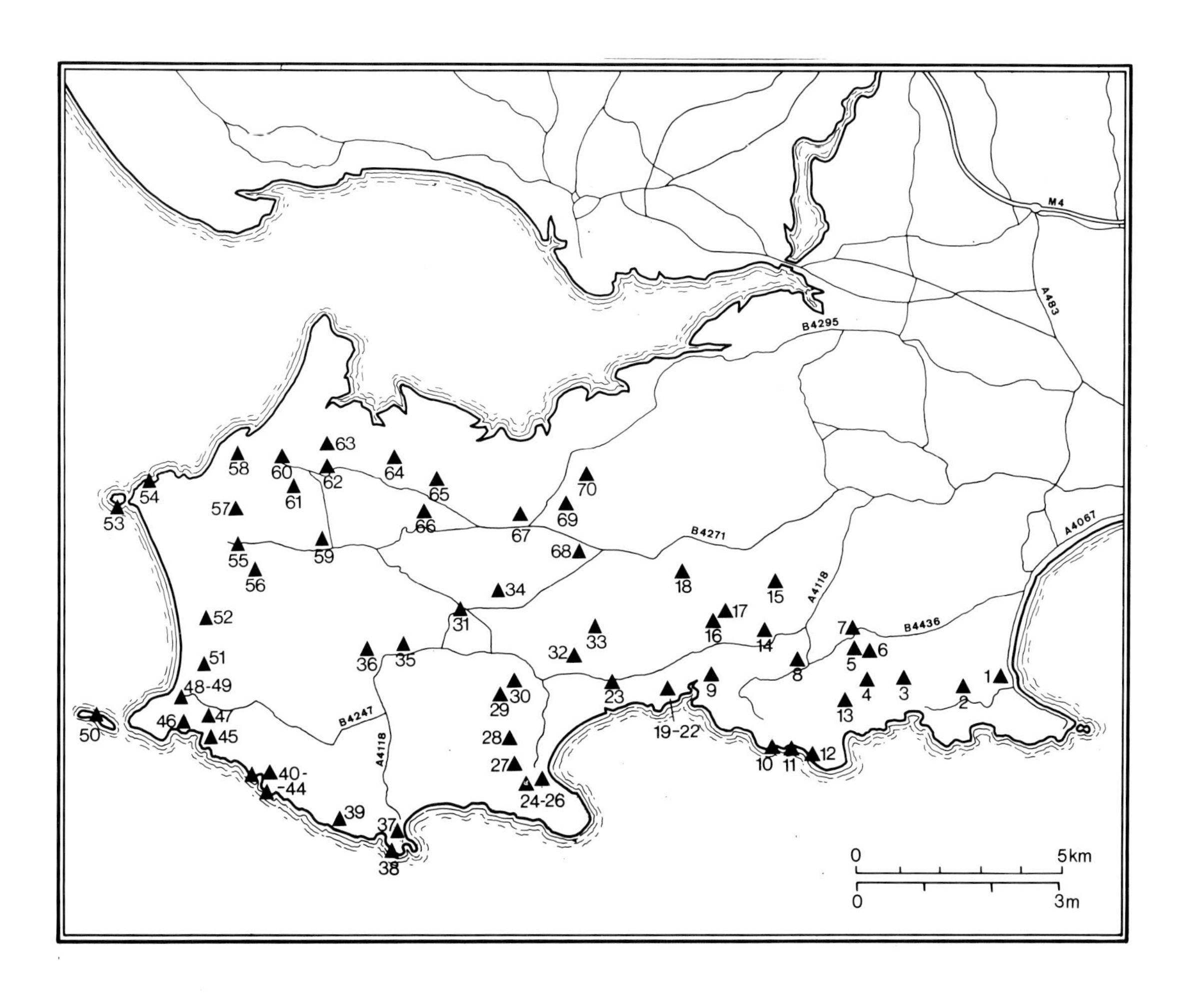

SWANSEA TO PORT EYNON

From the city centre the A4067 follows the sweep of Swansea bay west towards Oystermouth and Mumbles, by-passing a tiny stone bridge near the entrance to Clyne Valley Country Park. This ancient looking single arch bridge spans the Black Pill stream, and is now only used by pedestrians. Although there is a tradition that it was built by the Romans, it probably dates from the 18th century, and marks the position of the main coast road prior to modern improvements.

Oystermouth (1) is said to have been named after the shellfish once gathered here in abundance, but perhaps it was the nearest the English speaking settlers could get to pronouncing the Welsh name of Ystum-llwynarth. In the Dark Ages the place was remembered as the scene of a miraculous event in the life of St Illtyd. The 9th century monk Nennius wrote of a 'wonder in Gower, the altar in the place called Llwynarth, that is suspended by the will of God'. According to the story, while St Illtyd was meditating in a cave on the shore, he witnessed the approach of a boat guided by two men. On board was the body of a holy man above which floated a stone altar. In accordance with the holy man's wishes before his death, St Illtyd arranged the burial and later built a church around the sepulchre.

Isaac Hamon, the 17th century Gower antiquarian, recorded a curious folk-tale about a group of travellers who lived in St Illtyd's cave, and spent their time making small coloured bricks. 'Part of the churchyard was formerly paved with small bricks like dices ... of divers colours as red, white, yellow' wrote Hamon. In fact the 'dice' are the remains of a mosaic floor, and along with the discovery of coins in the last century, clearly indicate that there was a Roman building here. Fragments of the mosaic unearthed during rebuilding work on the church in 1860 are displayed inside.

Nennius' story about St. Illtyd raises the possibility that the church may have been established in the Dark Ages as an Early Christian centre. Could it have developed from the private chapel of a late Roman villa? Or is the proximity of the church and villa pure coincidence? The remaining Medieval part of All Saints Church now forms the south aisle of a grand Victorian edifice. It is a typical building of the 13th or 14th century consisting of a chancel, nave and west tower, a plan which is repeated in most of the Gower churches. Photographs taken before the building was extended in 1860 show a blocked arch in the north wall of the nave, which probably led into a demolished transept or side-chapel.

A short distance away on a hill overlooking the village and church stand the remains of *Oystermouth castle.* This has everything a castle enthusiast could want; towers, battlements, winding stairs, gloomy passages and haunted dungeons. Isaac Hamon was evidently impressed with what he saw in the 1690's, 'there is in this parish a very spacious Castle haveing many dry Roomes, vaults and sellers in it, with staires, towers and walkes

Fig. A: Oystermouth Castle in the 12th century.

Fig. B: Early 13th century.

Fig. C:
Later 13th century.

Fig. D:
Early 14th century.

very firm, in some arches there are flowers and coates of armes painted in divers colours'. The wall paintings can no longer be traced, but the intervening 300 years have had little effect on the durable limestone walls, and Oystermouth is the most intact castle in Gower. It is also the most complex, as any visitor exploring the warren of rooms and towers will appreciate. Despite the confusing layout, the development of the castle can be fairly accurately traced, although the times at which each part was built are less clear.

Henry de Beaumont gave the manor of Oystermouth to his follower William de Londres, lord of Ogmore, and a castle was built to defend his hold upon the territory. The site chosen was a steep rocky knoll which acted as a natural motte, and with the abundance of good building stone it is possible that the defences may have been of masonry from the start. Embedded within the surviving ruins on the very summit of the rock is an oblong keep, similar in size to the one at Ogmore, and also probably the work of William or his son, Maurice. Only the much-repaired basement survives of this, and the crude stonework contrasts with the better laid masonry of the upper floors. Probably the main living accommodation was on the first floor, above a basement store, and reached by an external stair (Fig. A). Evidently William didn't think much of his castle's strength, for when a Welsh army attacked Gower in 1116, he sneaked off, leaving his possessions, livestock and soldiers behind!

By the 13th century Oystermouth has passed under the control of the main lords of Gower, and after another Welsh raid in 1215, the De Breos clan began an ambitious rebuilding scheme. The keep was remodelled and a three-storey block was added to the north side. The ground floor rooms were converted into residential chambers, with large fireplaces in the central dividing wall. This work can be distinguished by the use of red stones for the arches of the doors and windows. In the middle of the west wall a curious winding stair was built, which could only be reached from the principal first floor apartments, and led down to a vaulted cellar under the keep. At ground level there is a dark passage which leads around the stairwell, but does not communicate with it. In this phase the castle may have looked something like figure B.

Next to be built was the north-west wing, a three-storey block awkwardly tagged on to one corner of the keep. This may have been intended to increase the accommodation, but at a later date it was converted into a garderobe (toilet) block, with vaulted rooms at different levels to the original floors. The drawing of this phase (Fig. C) shows the builders starting work on the west block, which when completed had vaulted storerooms on the ground floor and a large residential chamber above. King Edward I came to Oystermouth in December 1284, and it was at a partially completed fortress such as this that he stayed.

In the early years of the 14th century work began on a massive buttressed tower adjoining a corner of the keep. On the ground floor there was a kitchen, a residential chamber on the first floor, and on the top level a large chapel from which the tower has gained its name. The fine traceried windows of the chapel were reconstructed from fragments found during restoration work in the 1840's, and form a striking contrast with the more spartan details elsewhere in the castle. It was only after the chapel tower was finished that the surviving curtain walls were built, and all the various buildings linked up to form an almost continuous wall-walk. The gap between the north-west and the west blocks was filled in with yet another residential wing, with amenable chambers on three floors (Fig. D).

The gatehouse, Osytermouth Castle.

This emphasis on building the domestic quarters before the defensive perimeter is in total contrast to castle building practice in Wales, and perhaps suggests that Oystermouth was never viewed by the Lords of Gower as a front-line fortress. This would explain the missing gate-towers which have so puzzled historians for years. Visitors approaching the castle will see that on either side of the entrance there are curving wall faces which were clearly intended to form the inner sides of two round towers flanking the gate. Although some people think they were built and later demolished, it is more probable that they were planned, but never completed. It is significant that while there are doors leading from the castle into the towers at ground level, there are none on the upper floors. By the time work was nearing completion on the outer defences the political situation in Wales had changed; the native princes had been defeated, and things had settled down to the extent that the building scheme at Oystermouth was abandoned.

This was not the end of the castle's military life though; rebellion flared up in the early 15th century, and Gower was for a time controlled by Owain Glyndŵr. During the Civil War (1642-48) the castle was briefly reoccupied, and the large windows of the chapel tower were partially walled-up for the use of muskets, but there is no evidence of the extensive demolition Cromwell ordered to be carried out at other captured Royalist strongholds, and it may be that the castle never posed a serious military threat during the War. From then on the story is one of neglect and ruin. 'An old decayed castle' is how Oystermouth was described in 1650, and by the following century the site was beginning to draw visitors and antiquarians. Repairs were carried out in the first half of the 19th century by the owner, the Duke of Beaufort, and now, following further restoration work, the castle is open to the public during the summer months.

For a kilometre or two beyond Oystermouth the undulating landscape of the peninsula has been almost hidden beneath a maze of residential streets and houses, evidence of the popularity of Langland and Caswell bays among the city dwellers during the last hundred years. Isaac Hamon referred to an important lost Prehistoric site in this area, a pair of standing stones known as the 'Hoarstones', which were five and eight feet high, and stood about twenty yards apart in a cornfield. A more recent loss to the urban growth was *Nottage Farm*, (2) which lay close to the B4593 between the hamlets of Newton and Langland. Though the house had been extended over the years, the original early 17th century part survived virtually intact.

A restored view of Nottage Farm, Oystermouth.

There was only a single room on the ground floor, heated by a fireplace in a massive projecting chimney stack. The entrance was through a large porch containing a winding stair leading up to the loft.

Caswell Bay is so popular with summer visitors that trying to find a parking space here can be something of an ordeal. There is a small Iron Age hillfort on the west side of the bay, but the site is very overgrown and is not the most impressive example in Gower. The most important archeological site in the Caswell area lies about a kilometre inland and can be reached either by walking through Bishops Wood, or along a footpath from Oldway, village off the B4436. The ruins of *Caswell Chapel* (3) and pilgrimage centre are almost hidden from view behind a screen of bushes at the head of the valley. St Mary's chapel can be identified fairly easily, with its single upstanding gable wall pierced by a ragged opening marking the remains of the large east window. The rest of the walls have been reduced to foundations. A short distance to the north is a small square building which has been identified as a priest's house, although the absence of a fireplace suggests that it had a non-domestic function. When William Morgan visited and partly excavated the site in the 1890's, the east gable of the house was still standing.

Just beyond this building a small spring tricking out of a stone-lined opening in the hillside marks the site of St Peter's well. Morgan's diggings revealed the foundations of substantial building constructed around the spring, perhaps a well-chamber like the ones still to be seen at Penrhys (Rhondda), and Cwm Maelwg (Margam). Not enough evidence survives to indicate the age of the buildings, nor whether they are all contemporary, but they certainly formed a religious site under the control of the parish church of Bishopston. Apart from Morgan's excavation report, the only other source of information is Isaac Hamon, who was familiar with the site and described the well building 200 years before it was dug up; 'St Peters well is very firm walled and stone benches and pavement belonging to it, it never friezeth, it continueth the stream be the weather wet or dry'. He also mentioned another well here, dedicated to St John. 'Neare to these welles standeth an old religious house, but ruinated, and a chapell dedicated to the virgin Mary, to which place in old time was great resort'.

About a kilometre to the west in an almost identical setting on the edge of a dry valley, is the remains of *Backingstone chapel* (4). This sad little ruin stands in a field beside a signposted footpath from Pyle village to the Bishopston valley. Only two ivy-covered walls stand to their original height, but the remaining foundations show the chapel to have been a single-roomed building similar in size to the 'priest's house' at Caswell. In the Middle Ages Bishopston church held sanctuary land in this vicinity, and the little chapel might have been a refuge associated with that ancient privilege. Isaac Hamon, however, thought that the chapel belonged 'to an ancient built house called Backinstone', which might suggest instead it was used by the owners of the nearby house. Today, Backingstone is a modern farm, but for years one of the oldest houses on the peninsula mouldered away unrecognised in the farmyard. The Royal Commission on Ancient & Historical Monuments had barely finished a survey of the building in 1983 when it was demolished by the landowner. A sad loss.

The Commision's survey revealed that the house was one of the few to survive which retained all the main architectural features of the region such as round headed doorways, an outshut for a bed-cupboard, and stone winding stairs beside the entrance. It was built in the early 16th century and contained an outer room with a cross-passage, a large hall, and a parlour; there were also two large chambers on the first floor. Being of such an early date the house had details which recalled the Medieval concern for security; all the doors had wooden drawbars, the windows were small, and there was even an indoor privy in a little turret!

From here, the most scenic route to Bishopston is along the dry valley below Backinstone, past the site of a 19th century lead mine and Guzzle Hole cave, where the underground river can be glimpsed. Near the top end of the valley, on the western side, is another example of Gower vernacular architecture, fortunately still surviving, though incorporated into a range of farmbuildings. *Great Kittle Farm* (5) is privately owned, but a public footpath from the B4436 at Kittle Green leads along the edge of the valley and right past the house. The small grey building was built towards the end of the 16th century, and has the typical early features of round headed doors, a bed-cupboard outshut, and a stone stair rising over the entrance passage.

Bishopston Church (6)

The modern village of Bishopston has grown up on the hilltop overlooking the valley, leaving the old church very much to itself in the wooded dell below. There is a strong tradition that the earliest church was founded in the 6th century AD by St Teilo of Llandaff, and in Medieval documents the place is referred to as Lann Merguallt and Llandeilo Ferwallt, names which recall St Teilo and Mergualdus, the first head of the Celtic community. Llandaff's jurisdiction over the manor of Bishopston survived until this century. There is, unfortunately, no physical evidence to back up the documentary origin of Bishopston, for unlike the other Gower churches of Llanmadoc, Llangennith and Llangyfelach, no Early Christian carved stones have been found here. The fabric of the church is certainly no earlier than the 12th century, and the oldest part is probably the tower, which has a Norman style round-headed window in the south wall. The plain pointed arches of the windows and a blocked priest's door in the chancel appear to be early 13th century, while the main body of the church was rebuilt at a later date (probably in the 14th century). Over the entrance to the porch is a stone inscribed with the date 1851, which commemorates the first major restoration of St Teilo's church; there were further repairs in 1927. The Rood loft survived until the last century, and so, too, did the thatched roof which was once a common feature in Gower. Fortunately part of the church is still

Pennard church: a 13th century window with re-used 12th century stonework.

roofed over with six much-repaired timber trusses which probably date back to the rebuilding of the nave. They are of a type known as an 'arch-brace', shaped like a broad A, with the cross-beam (or collar) supported on the underside by curving struts.

Beyond the church the Murton to Bishopston road rejoins the B4436, and where this road begins to climb the west side of the valley, a few cracks and fissures can be seen in the cliff on the right. This is all that remains of the *Kittle Hill Cave* (7), which was quarried away in 1926 soon after it was discovered. A brief excavation there brought to light animal bones and a quantity of charcoal, indicating human occupation at some time in the past.

Pennard Church (8)
Just past the village of Kittle the traveller reaches a prominent junction where the B4436 makes a sharp right turn towards Parkmill, and joins the main south coast road (A4118). Here beside the junction stands the parish church of Pennard, in all respects a typical Gower village church except that it lacks a village! The reason for this is that the original Norman settlement lay 2km further west, and sand storms in the later Middle Ages rendered it uninhabitable. It seems likely that the existing building was designed to replace the older church, but the evidence is far from conclusive, and there may have been a church here at an early date. In any event, the present church only achieved parochial status in the 16th century when the vicar decided to abandon the original site.

The surviving details suggest that St Mary's was constructed in the 14th century, although one of the chancel windows has Norman carving, presumable re-used from the older church. The plan comprises the usual chancel and nave, with an added porch and vestry, and a small tower at the west end. This tower is more like an over-large bellcote, and the unusual double corbelled parapet gives it a rather top-heavy appearance. The exterior walls bear the marks of a blocked north door into the nave and, according to local folk-lore, when in use this door would have been left open during christenings so that an exorcised evil spirit could flee from the church. In fact, opposing doorways are a common feature of Medieval architecture particularly domestic buildings, such as Glebe Farm (62). The interior has been well restored and many of the original features have been lost, but the old timber beam supporting the present gallery may well have formed part of the Rood loft.

Pennard Castle (9)
The old village and castle lie on the edge of the burrows beside the Pennard valley, and can be reached by following the road past St Mary's church towards Southgate. Several footpaths cross the dunes from the golf-course club house (but watch out for low-flying golf balls!). There is a more scenic route from the A4118 at Parkmill which follows the river downstream, and from this direction the castle appears as a dramatic ruin perched on the edge of a cliff.

Pennard Castle was probably established soon after the Normans invaded Gower, since the village church is listed among the endowments to Llangennith Priory (founded by 1119). The first castle was an earth and timber ringwork defended by a deep ditch and bank on the landward flank. Late in the 13th century (perhaps around 1300) William de Breos III replaced the timber defences with a thin stone wall on the line of the ringwork bank, and built a large gatehouse on the east side leading into the adjacent village. This gatehouse was a two-storeyed building with an entrance pass-

Pennard Castle.

A reconstruction drawing of Pennard Castle as it may have looked in the 14th century.

age defended by a portcullis and wooden gate, and set between two rounded towers; in effect a cruder and smaller version of the great gatehouses still to be seen at Caerphilly, Neath and Llanstephan. The curtain wall was far too flimsy ever to have supported a parapet, and so beams were inserted through the wall to form a timber walk-way. On the surviving stretch of the north wall there is a garderobe and a round turret, and next to it is a square tower built out onto the cliff edge. Within the enclosure the main accommodation was provided by a free-standing hall block, which belonged to the ringwork phase of the castle. This single-storeyed stone building contained a central hall, with store rooms at one end and a private room, or 'solar', at the other. The roof was probably thatched, and the only heating was provided by a hearth on the floor of the hall. The smoke would have escaped through a roof vent, or through the doors and unglazed windows. A visit to one of the recreated Medieval buildings at Cosmeston in South Glamorgan will give a good impression of living conditions in such a dark and smoky hall.

Under the dunes beyond the castle gate lies the lost village of Pennard, buried overnight by a magical sandstorm according to legend. But it was a gradual encroachment of sand that made the area less habitable, a phenomenon which affected other parts of South Wales including Kenfig, Margam and Rhossili. As early as 1317 there is documentary evidence of sand-burrows in the vicinity, and when a valuation of church property was compiled in 1535 the Vicar of Pennard claimed that 'the said churche and the vicaraige with all the glebe landes ... is utterly and clearly destroyed and overgon with the dryfte sandes of the see'. By 1650 the castle was described as 'desolate and ruinous, and soe long time unrepayred that scarsely there remayneth one whole wall'. This is a slight exaggeration, for when the topographers Samuel and Nathaniel Buck published an engraving of the castle in 1741 they showed the ruin largely as it appears today. The adjoining village, however, has fared much worse and today only a jagged stump of the church wall rises above ground to mark the final resting place of old Pennard.

Pennard Bone Caves

The limestone cliffs which helped protect Pennard castle from attack also provided the local populace with places of refuge centuries before the Normans set foot in Britain. Along the seaward face of the National Trust owned coastline there are around a dozen caves and rock shelters which can be reached from the car-park at the end of the Southgate road. Some of the caves have been washed clean of any archeological deposits by the rising post-glacial sea level, but others, such as Bosco's Den and Crow Hole, have produced the remains of mammoth, rhinoceros, hippopotamus, reindeer, wolf, and other animals. In most cases the remains of the larger creatures would have been dragged into the caves by predatory wolves and scavenging hyenas. Two of the Pennard caves, however, were home to a different kind of animal.

The dark entrance to Minchin Hole.

Minchin Hole (10) lies at the foot of the cliffs about 450m south-east of the car-park, and can be reached by a rough track that descends into Foxhole bay and curves around the headland towards the left. Inside the dark chamber an uneven floor of stalagmite and breccia rises steeply up to the back of the cave, where the rock walls have been covered with natural calcite formations. Various excavations have been carried out here since the middle of the last century, and the finds include the remains of warm and cold period animals, human bones and flints (which may have come from a Prehistoric burial) and metalwork of Iron Age date.

Between 1946 and 1959 excavations concentrated on four hearth areas which had been used by a native group during Roman times. The wealth of finds cover a period from the 2nd century AD to the early 5th century AD, and included over 750 pieces of pots, jars, beakers, dishes, bowls and other utensils. The inhabitants of this dark and draughty hole owned fine metal brooches and bracelets, bone combs, Roman coins and, most surprising of all, a set of at least eight delicately carved bone spoons. The image that springs to mind is of a Celtic family huddled around a glowing hearth in the midst of the gloom, eating food out of clay pots with fine cutlery. An incongruous scene perhaps, for it is more probable that the spoons were intended for the market place than the Minchin Hole dinner table! The excavations also uncovered evidence of small-scale metalworking and wool production.

Although these clues provide some idea of the belongings and skills of the cave dwellers, they do not indicate how many people lived here, nor whether Minchin Hole was occupied continuously or just at certain times of the year. Another mystery surrounds the presence of three coins discovered in 1948, which had been deposited in the cave around the middle of the 9th century AD. One is a penny of Ecgbert of Wessex (802-839) and the others are deniers of French and Italian origin. The coins are likely to have formed part of a Viking hoard and may conceivably have been hidden, or lost, by a group of raiders sheltering here.

Bacon Hole (11) is the second cave which has produced evidence of human occupation, and it lies about a third of the way up the cliff 600m east of Minchin Hole. The huge cave mouth is formed of overhanging sheets of limestone and breccia, leading to a low and broad chamber. Those armed with a torch can just make out the last vestiges of a metal grill which once sealed off a small side chamber near the back of the cave. This was set up in 1912 to protect what was then believed to be the only examples of Paleolithic cave art in Britain. A photograph taken at the time shows a series of parallel red streaks covered with a thin layer of stalagmite on the rock face.

Bacon Hole could have been dramatically transformed into an archeological showpiece, like the bone cave at Dan-yr-Ogof in the upper Swansea valley, but unfortunately interest in the 'paintings' waned when the marks began to fade away. It is now generally accepted that the marks were natual formations of red iron oxide, although there is a story that a salvage crew used the cave to store paint many years ago; the marks do look suspiciously as though someone has cleaned a paint brush on the wall!

More orthodox finds have proved that Bacon Hole afforded shelter to Celtic families before, and during, the Roman occupation. The most notable find was the remains of a decorated clay bowl which had been imported from Brittany in the 4th or 5th century BC. Another souvenir of a nameless visitor to the cave was a little flute, carved from a bird bone, and lost or discarded here by a child sometime in the Middle Ages.

High Pennard Promontory Fort (12)

East of Bacon Hole the cliffs rise more than 90m above sea level, the highest point on the entire Gower and Glamorgan coast. Here on a promontory beside the great rocky escarpment of Pwlldu Head, a Celtic family built a fortified settlement around two thousand years ago. The summit of the promontory is divided in two by natural cliffs, so that the area enclosed by the man-made defences is on separate levels. A single bank and ditch cuts off the lower part, where two hut sites were found during excavations here in 1939. The upper level is more effectively defended by a prominent double line of banks and ditches on the landward side.

Excavations concentrated on the innermost rampart, and a timber gateway was located, along with a 'guard hut' beside the entrance. A more unusual discovery was a drain and pit dug into the bedrock, which seems to have been designed to catch surface water for drinking purposes. Animal bones and shellfish remains give an idea of the diet of the settlers, and the chance find of a spindlewhorl indicates that some weaving was carried out. Fragments of pottery dating from the late 1st-2nd century AD suggest that the fort was occupied soon after the Roman invasion.

High Pennard promontory fort was sufficiently well known for the cartographer Emanuel Bowen to include it on his 1729 map of South Wales, though it is misleadingly drawn as a star-shaped artillery fort!

From the clifftop eyrie of High Pennard, the coast path descends to Pwlldu Bay where it connects with the trail leading up the Bishopston Valley. About 1km along the valley there is a sharp right turn, and on the ridge above the bend is an overgrown *promontory fort* (13). Two lines of rubble banks and rock-cut ditches protected the level approach from the east, and the only entrance was an easily defended path between the ends of the ramparts and the steep slope. The fort was excavated around the same time as High Pennard, and was similarly occupied by a Celtic family during Roman times. A hut was located just behind the inner rampart, but despite selective digs in the remainder of the enclosure no other dwelling sites came to light.

We have now almost arrived back at Bishopston Church, a circuitous tour of about 10km. The way on to the rest of the Peninsula is via a right hand turn at Pennard Church, and then left at the junction with the A4118. The road snakes past the boundary wall of Kilvrough Manor, 18th century seat of the Dawkins family, and then dips down into Ilston Cwm. The popular Gower Inn stands guard at the entrance to the valley, and marks the start of a 2km path through the woods to the parish church. The less energetic can reach this destination by car along a signposted road from Parkmill village.

Ilston chapel (14)

On the right hand side of the path about 400m along the valley can be seen a few ruined walls within the remains of an enclosure, all that survives of the first Baptist church in Wales. When the site was tidied up in 1928 a plaque was unveiled by Lloyd George commemorating the building of this chapel by John Miles, rector of Ilston, in 1649. There is however, some confusion over the place, since there was also a Medieval shrine hereabouts known as Trinity Well or St Kenyd's chapel. Writing at the end of the 17th century, Isaac Hamon appears to suggest that the two buildings were still standing then; 'There is in ye southern part of this parish a well called Trinity Well, by the same there is an old religious house and a chapell, but uncovered'. By that Hamon means the buildings were roofless and in decay. The well he mentions is probably the spring that still flows from the south side of the ruin. Miles' predecessor, John Houghton, is also claimed to have built Ilston chapel, using stones taken from the Medieval shrine. The traditionalist Houghton was ousted in favour of the puritan Miles during the Commonwealth period, but with the restoration of the monarchy in 1660 he regained his former post. John Miles and his followers packed their bags and emigrated to America, where they founded the town of Swanzey in Massachusetts.

Ilston Church (15)
St Illtyd's church lies on a sloping site between the little river and the hillside, a setting which recalls Bishopston and this too, is believed to be a Dark Age foundation. The plan consists of the usual nave and chancel, with a porch, tower and vestry all added to the south side. Restoration work in the last century may have preserved the fabric, but it has also removed many original features which would help date the various parts of the building. All the windows are modern; the arches of the chancel, tower, and blocked north door of the nave are of a type that could belong to the 13th, 14th or 15th centuries. A clue to the date is provided by a curious feature in the south wall of the tower, namely a square cupboard topped with a triangular recess. The same structure can be seen at St Mary's church Pennard (8), which was probably built in the early 14th century and suggests that the Ilston tower is of the same age.

Perhaps the most likely stages in the development of Ilston are that the old Norman church was rebuilt in the 13th century as a single rectangular building, now the nave. Perhaps the tower was next to be built, in the 14th century, followed by the small chancel which is squeezed in between the nave and the steep hillside. The porch is a late Medieval addition, and the vestry was probably built after the Reformation. The off-centre chancel arch and other eccentricities of the plan can no doubt be blamed on the restricted site, which may have been quite adequate for a Dark Age oratory, but not for a large Medieval church.

Ilston is the only Gower church to retain a complete pre-19th century roof; there are six blackened trusses in the nave, of a much simpler design than the arch-braced type seen at Bishopston. They may be contemporary with the nave, but the two trusses in the chancel are later, and resemble those found in houses of 15th and 16th century date. The nave contains a number of 18th century memorial stones, and an early 16th century bell of Bristol manufacture bearing the inscription 'Sancte Thome ora pro nobis' ('St Thomas pray for us'). There is a tomb recess in the north wall of the chancel, but the effigy or grave slab has unfortunately not survived.

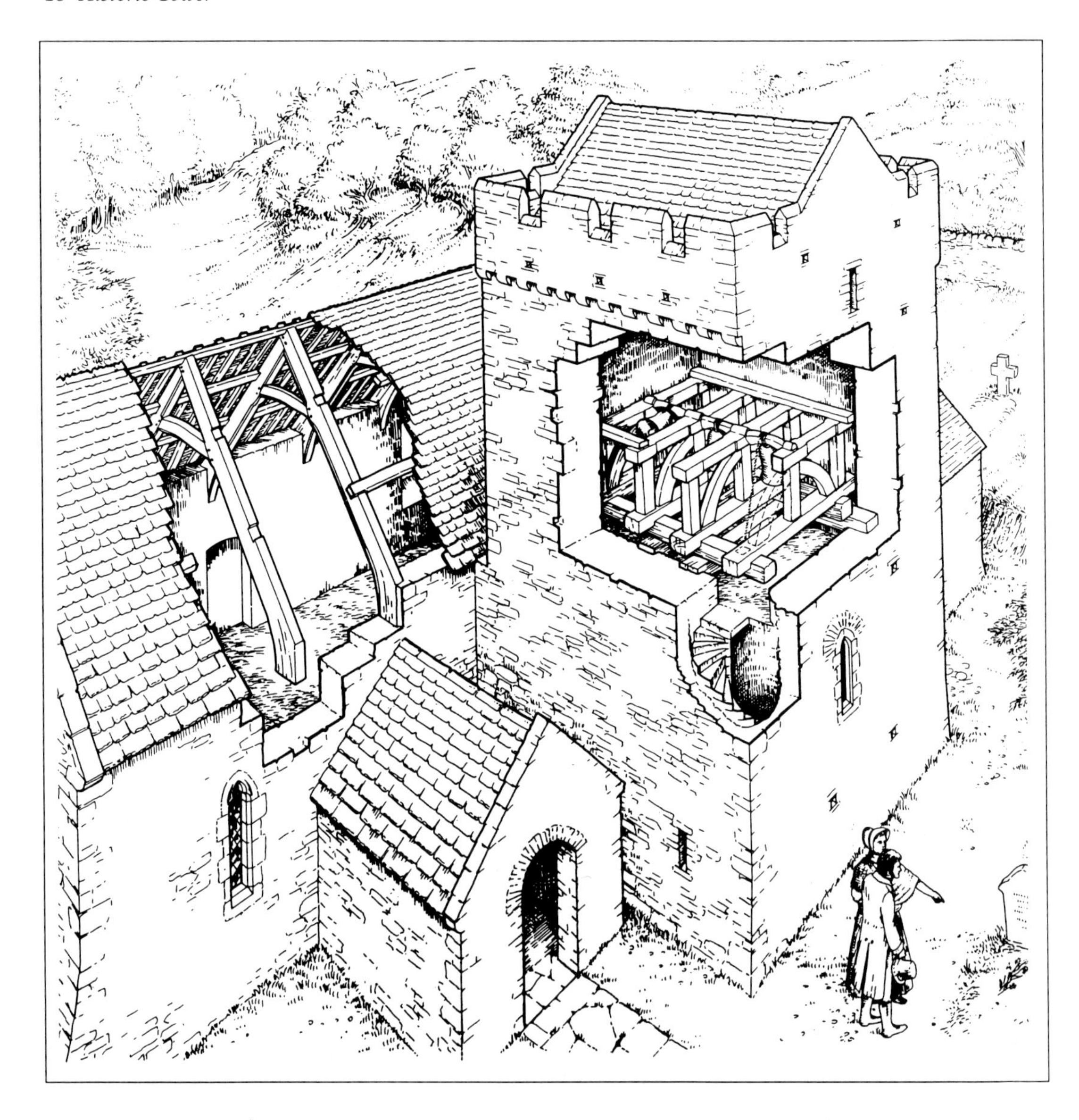

Cutaway drawing of Ilston Church, c.1850.

The vaulted ground floor of the tower has now been sealed off from the nave, but it was originally open and used as a transept or side chapel. A tortuously narrow stair in one corner climbs up to a single chamber where a latticework of beams support two bells cast in the early 18th century. All the timbers are marked with Roman numerals which helped the carpenters reassemble the prefabricated structure after each piece had been dragged up to the top. From the outside the unrestored tower looks much older than the rest of the building, and there is a tradition that it was used by local people for defence during troubled times, as a sort of 'mini castle'. But there is little evidence to support this, since there is no access to the roof and the battlements are purely decorative.

Park Cwm

Back at the Gower Inn, it is only a short distance along A4118 to the little village of Parkmill and the start of another woodland valley trail. The parking here is limited at the best of times, and in summer the village can be packed with day-trippers. Just opposite Shepherds Store is a signposted footpath leading over the river and through the woods to Three Cliffs bay, passing close to Pennard Castle. In the village itself the old watermill has recently been restored and opened to the public; it dates from the early 19th century, but probably occupies the site of a late Medieval mill.

Park Cwm, or Green Cwm, is the wooded valley which winds inland behind the village for about 2 miles. It was carved out by a river thousands of years ago, before the honeycombed bedrock drew the water under-gound, so that for much of its length the valley is 'dry'. The place-name and its more familiar variant Park le Breos refers to the great deer park which the lords of Gower established here in the Middle Ages. Almost 2000 acres of land were enclosed with an earthwork bank to prevent the animals from escaping, and the remains of the boundary can still be traced on the ground and on large scale OS maps. Many deer parks continued in use well into the 17th century as a necessary adjunct to a grand house, but Park Cwm fell into disuse by the Reformation, and the antiquarian Rice Merrick wrote (c.1588) of 'an ancient lodge house ... sometime imparked with a wall and pale, but long time past disparked'.

A view along the forecourt of the chambered cairn at Park Cwm.

Park Cwm Long Cairn (16)
Merrick, nor any other antiquary, made any mention of this impressive Prehistoric monument, probably for the very simple reason that no-one knew of its existance until the late 19th century. This Neolithic tomb lies in a fenced-off enclosure beside the path, about half a mile beyond Parkmill. It now looks virtually complete, lacking only the large slabs which would have roofed over the burial chambers and connecting passages; but this is the result of careful restoration work in 1961.

The site was discovered by accident in 1869 when workmen constructing a nearby road decided to plunder the cairn mound for building stones; What they found brought the work to a halt. Three years later, the diarist Francis Kilvert visited Parc Cwm and gave a somewhat fanciful description of the remains; 'These graves were uncovered a few years ago and there were found in some of them skeletons sitting upright'; hardly likely! In fact the excavators wrote that the bones were 'much broken and in no regular arrangement', as one might expect in a ruined 5000-year-old tomb. The remains of as many as twenty four people, and pieces of Neolithic pottery, were found. The Park Cwm long cairn belongs to a specific group of Neolithic monuments known as the 'Severn Cotswold' tombs, named after their distribution in the Cotswolds and Severn Valley areas. The characteristic feature of this class is a series of burial chambers branching off the entrance passage, which is accessed from a *forecourt* at one end of the oblong cairn. Here, a funnel-shaped forecourt at the south end of the mound leads to a low, slab-lined passageway, with four side chambers. The tomb is now roofless and open to the sky, but originally there would hae been roofing slabs covered with stones, so that a Neolithic tribesman would have had to crawl along a pitch black tunnel to deposit any bones.

Kilvert called the site 'the Graves of the Unknown', and it is sometimes referred to as 'The Giant's Grave', names (like Arthur's Stone at Reynoldston) which hint at some legendary origin, but which can be no older than the late 19th century.

On the wooded hilltop just west of the tomb is an oval earthwork enclosure, which is probably the remains of an Iron Age homestead. However, the place-name 'Church Hill' is rather puzzling, since there is no church here, and its location might suggest a connection with the Medieval deer park.

Cathole Cave (17)
A long time after the last Neolithic farmer was laid to rest in the tomb, the new Bronze Age tribes found another place in Park Cwm to bury their dead. Instead of the usual practice of sealing the remains under a round cairn on a ridge or hilltop, they placed the bones in funerary urns and then buried them in the dark recesses of Cathole cave.

The cave can be found on the right hand side of the path, behind some trees, about 200m past the tomb, and a modern flight of steps leads up to the twin entrances. Inside there is a single large chamber, with a dark cul-

Inside Cathole Cave.

de-sac passage at the rear. Cathole had been used by Prehistoric Man long before the Bronze Age, as the results of excavations in 1864, 1958 and 1968 have proved. The earliest flint tools were associated with Ice Age animal remains, and one flint may belong to the 'Upper Perigordian' period of the Upper Palaeolithic about 26,000BC. Most of the stone tools and the waste products from their manufacture belong to the 'Creswellian' period 10,000 to 8,000BC when the ice cap was beginning to retreat. Finds of Mesolithic date, 8,000 to 4,000BC show that Cathole was again used by nomadic hunters, tracking down their prey on the great plains now lost beneath the waters of the Bristol Channel.

Archaeologists believe that Cathole was a 'transit camp' used on hunting expeditions by the same group which also stayed at Paviland (40), Long-hole (39) and North Hill Tor (63) caves. Potsherds of Medieval date indicate that the cave was still used for some purpose, at a time when Park Cwm was the jealously guarded preserve of the Norman aristocracy. And even in comparatively recent times, Isaac Hamon claimed that people were frightened to pass the cave because it was the hideout of a gang of robbers!

There is yet another cave in Park Cwm which was utilised by the Bronze Age tribes, but this is not really accessible to the public since it is part of an extensive underground system, the domain of the experienced potholer. *Tooth Cave* (18) lies near the head of the valley, just inside the forestry boundary on the right hand side and a small metal door at the base of some

A view along the entrance passage into the ruined Neolithic tomb of Penmaen Burrows.

rocks prevents access. Excavations in the early 1960's uncovered flint and bone tools, potsherds, and the skeletal remains of at least eight people, of Early Bronze Age date. Clearly Tooth Cave, like Cathole and the Llangennith Culver Hole (54) was used mainly as a sepulchre, the ready-made equivalent of the earlier Neolithic burial chambers.

Returning now to Parkmill, the A4118 climbs out of the valley and soon passes through the modern village of Penmaen, where there is a small car park and a signposted footpath leading down to the National Trust owned headland. The parish church of St John the Baptist stands guard at the approach to the village, and though it was built in the late Middle Ages it was extensively refurbished and enlarged in 1854-5. Inside there are several 17th and 18th century monuments including a notable gravestone of one Richard Davies (d.1623) who traced his descent from the Welsh princes. The stone shows the arms of the last native ruler of Glamorgan, Iestyn ap Gwrgant, impaled with the Mansel crest. The original settlement lay on the headland below the village, but was obliterated by drifting sands in the late Middle Ages; However, like Pennard just across the valley, the ruins of the more substantial buildings still survive above ground.

Old Penmaen church (19) was located in 1861 when a fragment of painted glass was discovered on a sand dune. The site was duly excavated and the outline of a simple chancel and nave building was laid bare. Beneath the floor of the chancel the remains of nine skeletons were found; six had been hastily buried in a single grave, and since the only entrance into the chancel had been blocked off, the excavators wondered if the skeletons were those of plague victims. A less gruesome discovery was a finely decorated bronze incense burner in the shape of the holy city of Jerusalem, this can now be seen in the Swansea Museum. The church can be identified as a sunken, stone-lined depression, on the left of the path, about 150m east of the entrance gate to the burrows.

A few dunes to the south-east is a monument entirely unconnected with the Medieval settlement, a ruined Neolithic *burial chamber* (20), which was here at least 3000 years before the Normans arrived. The survival of this relic so close to a Christian centre is surprising, and makes one wonder what the villagers made of their megalithic neighbour. There are many sites in Britain where churches hae been built on, or close to, Prehistoric monuments in an attempt to sanctify a pagan area. Knowlton in Dorset and Rudston in Humberside are well known, but Gower also has a second example at Knelston (35). Although much of the Penmaen tomb is missing and covered in sand, enough of its structure survives to place it in the Severn Cotswold group. A slab-lined passageway led to a central burial chamber, with additional compartments on the south and east sides. There was probably another on the north, so that the tomb originally had a cruciform plan. All trace of a surrounding cairn has been hidden by the drifting sand. When William Morgan excavated the site in 1893 a few fragments of pottery and human bones were found in the south chamber.

Castle Tower (21)

On the eastern edge of the burrows overlooking Threecliff Bay is the site of the Norman stronghold of Penmaen. This is the most accessible of the many ringworks in Gower and, thanks to excavations in 1960-61, we know more about its development than any of the other sites. In the early 12th century the castle occupied an oval area of headland enclosed on the landward side by a curving bank of rubble and stones, with an outer ditch. The entrance was through a 6m square timber gatetower, which probably had at least one upper floor, and seems to have acted much like a conventional 'keep'. The only other building in the courtyard was a small timber hall or tower. This first phase of occupation came to an end with the burning of the gatehouse, perhaps as the result of an enemy attack. The whole site was then remodelled and the earthwork defences strengthened. Although the gatehouse was never rebuilt, the entrance gap was narrowed to form a stone-walled passageway and the adjacent rampart was flattened, as if to act as a base for a wooden turret. Within the enclosure a crude hall was raised, which had low drystone walls and a thatch or turf roof (see reconstruction drawing). In plan, this building closely resembles the halls excavated at Rhossili (48) and Burry Holms (53), and proves that life for the privileged owner of a small castle could be just as basic as that endured by everyone else in the village. Archeological evidence suggests that the castle was

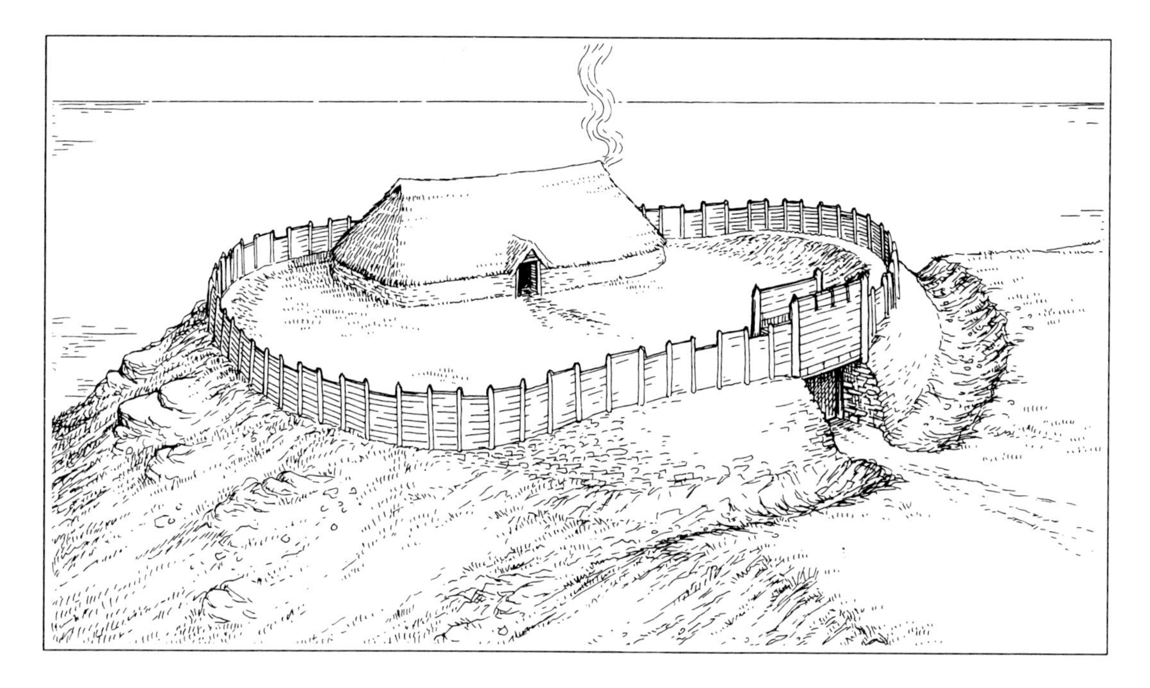

Reconstruction of Castle Tower, Penmaen, phase II.

abandoned early in the 13th century, no doubt due to Welsh attacks in 1215-1217 and attempts to expel the English settlers from Gower.

On level ground about 50m directly west of the castle there is a long, low mound with shallow side ditches, now almost hidden in the bracken and heather. This mysterious-looking object had the very mundane function of providing a suitable place for rabbits to dig their burrows. The rabbit was introduced into Britain by the Normans, and until the last century it was valued as a source of fresh meat and fur. Just as the economic importance of the humble pigeon is commemorated by huge stone dovecots at Oxwich (25), Penrice (30) and Port Eynon (38), so the coney has its monument in these so-called *pillow mounds*. Whether the Penmaen mound is Medieval or later is not known, but rabbits were certainly being farmed at Pennard in the 14th century, and Isaac Hamon mentioned warrens at Oxwich, Rhossili and Llanmadoc.

There is one more archeological site on Penmaen burrows to mention, a bone cave known as *Leather's Hole* (22) which is situated in Great Tor at the southernmost tip of the headland. Access is by a short, but difficult path over the gap between the two peaks, and then a rough scramble up and around to the left. The cave consists of a small series of passages and chambers leading deep into the rock. The bones of mammoth and rhinoceros were found here in the last century, but the only way these bulky animals could have got inside the cave would be in pieces, as food for hyaenas and wolves. Isaac Hamon mentioned that the cave was 'the working and lodging place of Robers clippe Coyners'; having spent a night in Leather's Hole some years ago I have every sympathy with the Tudor caveman!

From Penmaen Green the main road continues westwards between the gorse-covered slopes of Cefn Bryn and the curving expanse of Oxwich Bay. *Nicholaston Church* (23) is soon reached, a modern building on the site of a much older structure (which may also have replaced a nearby lost church). A drawing of the interior made prior to restoration in 1891 shows a plain and simple building with an earth floor and whitewashed walls. The round chancel arch suggests the church was built in the 12th century, though the single massive roof truss with a central cusped opening is much later, perhaps 15th century. The blocked up doorway of a disused rood loft could be seen, as well as faint traces of wall paintings. The present building contains one of the oldest bells in Gower, inscribed with the Dutch line 'I am cast in the year of Our Lord 1518', which is thought to have been brought from a shipwreck.

About a mile further on the traveller is confronted by the shattered walls and towers of an ancient fortress; but all is not what it seems. This is the

The interior of Nicholaston Church prior to 19th century restoration (based on a drawing in J. D. Davies's 'History of West Gower'.

lodge to the Penrice Castle estate, a fine example of the 18th-century taste for landscaped Gothick ruins. A left turn here leads down the hillside and across a marshy nature reserve to the village of Oxwich. This is one of the busiest resorts in the summer months, but a short walk along the coast path will bring you to a little haven of peace. *St Illtyd's Church* (24) lies in a quiet grove on the edge of the sea, a site reputedly hallowed for at least thirteen centuries. The existing building is no older than the 12th century and has the familiar plan of a chancel, nave and west tower. From the outside it is easy to see the joints in the walls which show that the original Norman building was extended westwards in the 16th century, with the ground floor of the tower acting as an entrance porch. This porch now contains two Medieval gravestones discovered during restoration work in the last century.

The small size of the chancel has led to some speculation that it may have been an Early Christian oratory, but there is little evidence for this. The east window is 14th century, but the walls and the narrow round headed chancel arch date from the 12th century and show how small and simple the Gower churches of the Norman period were. Llanmadoc, Penrice and Llangennith also have round arches of the same period. Within the chancel there is a richly decorated recess known as 'Doolamur's hole' which contains the effigies of an armed knight and his lady. This splendid monument is supposed to commemorate members of the De la Mare clan, but the style of the armour has been dated to the early 15th century when the manor of Oxwich had long been held by the Penres family. The effigies may be of Sir John Penres (d. 1410) and his wife, Margaret Fleming. Analysis of the monument

Oxwich Castle.

Reconstruction of Oxwich Castle.

has revealed it to be formed of sand grains cemented together with plaster, and covered with a painted plaster coat.

The rest of the interior has been extensively restored, and the nave has an impressive modern example of a 'Medieval' arch-braced roof. The finely painted Rood beam is modern too, but it gives a good impression of what this feature looked like in Medieval churches before the Reformation put paid to 'popish' imagery.

Oxwich Castle (25)
Although known as a 'castle', this huge ruin perched on the hilltop above the church is, in fact, the remains of a 16th century mansion. The battlements and turrets were never meant to repel invaders, just to impress upon all visitors the ostentatious wealth of the owners, and recall the departed splendour of the feudal age. There was a real castle here, it is mentioned in Medieval documents and the foundations have been excavated in the courtyard; there is even a length of walling inside the house which formed part of the earlier stronghold.

Virtually all of what survives today was built in the years 1520 to 1580 by the Mansels, a local family that rose to prominence during the reign of the Tudors. The Glamorgan historian Merrick, writing in the 1580's, claimed that Oxwich was 'lately re-edified or repaired by Sir Edward Mansel, Knight', and that his father, Sir Rice, had built part of the castle. Exactly who built what and when, has long been a source of debate, since the castle consists of two quite separate parts displaying different architectural details. There is a two-storeyed south wing used for many years as a farmhouse, and an adjoining courtyard enclosed by battlemented walls and a gatehouse. Just outside the courtyard there is a large beehive-shaped dovecot. Adjoining the south wing at right angles is a huge multi-storeyed east block, which is basically a long rectangular building with three tower-like projections at the rear.

The east block is one of the most remarkable Tudor buildings in Wales. At his heart lay the great hall, which occupied the first floor above the kitchens and vaulted basements. The hall was reached from the courtyard through a large porch which has entirely vanished except for the foundations (and so the appearance of the porch in the accompanying drawing is conjectural). At the high table end of the hall the Mansels' building ambitions become apparent. A grand staircase led up to a long gallery running the length of the building and lit by spacious windows. But the most remarkable feature of Oxwich is the six storey corner tower, the Tudor equivalent of a high-rise block, which could have accommodated a large number of retainers.

That the Tudor gentry relied on the support of what might be classed a private army, is highlighted by a dramatic incident of December 1557. In that month a French ship was wrecked in the bay, and the steward of Oxwich and some local men collected the booty and shared it out amongst themselves. When Sir George Herbert of Swansea heard of this, he decided that the goods should belong to the Earl of Worcester (then Lord of Gower), and marched off with a troop of men to Oxwich. The local houses were searched and the goods confiscated, then Sir George made his way to the Castle where he was confronted by the young Edward Mansel, his aunt Lady Anne, and their retainers. Heated words were exchanged, a scuffle broke out, and Lady Anne was struck on the head by a stone flung indiscriminately by one of Herbert's men. She collapsed, bleeding, to the ground and died a short time later. For his part in the affray, Sir George was merely fined by the Privy Council.

Some 17 years before this event, Sir Rice Mansel had purchased part of the large estate of the dissolved Cistercian Abbey at Margam, and began to build a new residence there. By the end of the 16th century this had become the main family seat, and the impressive tomb-effigies of the Mansels can be seen in the Abbey church. Oxwich was leased out to tenant farmers, and while the smaller and more covenient south wing was inhabited, the unwieldy east block was left to fall into ruin. The Castle is now cared for by CADW – Welsh Historic Monuments, and after years of conservation work it is open to the public during the summer months.

About 400m away from the Mansel's great palace stood another 16th century house that sadly has not been preserved for prosterity. *Oxwich Green Farm* (26) lay behind some modern houses on the south side of the

Green, and until recently survived as an overgrown, crumbling shell. Only a few architectural details remained to hint at the importance of this well-to-do farmer's home, which had been erected towards the end of the reign of Elizabeth I. The Royal Commission on Ancient and Historical Monuments carried out a detailed survey of the building, revealing it had a typical late-Medieval plan of an open hall, separated from a two-storeyed parlour wing by a cross-passage. The two huge chimney stacks set in the side walls, rather than the gables, is a feature more often found in houses of high standing.

After leaving the Castle, and before reaching Oxwich Green, there is a right-hand turn which leads along a narrow lane to Penrice village. Half a mile along the road curves past *Norton Farm* (27) where, in a field behind the buildings, can be seen a small earthwork enclosure. OS maps mark it simply as a 'settlement' – but is it Iron Age as some people think? The small size of the area enclosed, and the remains of an oblong building platform inside suggests it is a Medieval ringwork. Lying so close to Oxwich Castle, it may have been an early stronghold of the manor.

A short distance further along the lane and you pass the whitewashed walls of *Pitt house* (28), a privately-owned residence dating from the mid 17th century. Pitt displays the new trends in building plans that were filtering down from the grand Renaissance houses; the hall and parlour are sparated from the kitchen by an entrance lobby and stairwell that provided better circulation and greater privacy for the occupants. From the roadside the most obvious indications of the age of the building are the distinctive chimney stacks and several blocked stone windows. The inventory of Mary Bennett of Pitt (c.1700) has survived and makes interesting reading concerning the household goods a relatively well-off family owned by the end of the 17th century. The list includes pewter plates, flagons, candlesticks, 'one fryen pan' and even 'a chamber pott'. Mary's most prized possessions were her clothes, which were assessed at £5 (a sum which speaks volumes about the changing values of money)!

Penrice (29) is a place-name of Welsh origin but there is nothing here now to suggest that the village pre-dates the Norman invasion of Gower. It is a typical settlement of the feudal era, a little group of houses and cottages (sadly no longer thatched) huddled around the parish church of St Andrew and the earthworks of a large ringwork castle. That mine of information, Isaac Hamon, wrote that a great fair was held here on St Andrew's day, but that 'eversince ye year 1665 there hath been 3 fayres more kept, and a market upon friday'. Clearly the sleepy village was more populous and prosperous in olden days. This is also reflected in the scale of the parish church, one of the largest in Gower, and comprising a west tower, nave, chancel, north transept and south porch. The building was severely 'restored' by the Victorians and some of the walls and windows rebuilt; the few remaining original features suggest that the main body of the church dates from the late 12th century, with the porch and transept added in the

14th century. The size of the porch is quite surprising, it is larger than the transept, and was commodious enough to accommodate the Sunday school classes. The inner entrance is particularly noteworthy, for the original arched opening has been replaced with a smaller wooden door frame, the only one to survive in a Gower church.

The ringwork castle behind the village is on private land, and the dense covering of bushes makes any exploration impossible at present. The defences consist of an oval mound up to 45m across with a rampart around the edge, and an outer ditch. A gap on the north side of the bank marks the site of an entrance which, like Penmaen, was perhaps guarded by a wooden tower. Hamon refered to the castle as 'a great bullwarke called Mount y brwrch', a name which endures to this day as Mounty Bank or Mounty-borough.

Watermills played an important role in the rural economy of Gower, whether for grinding corn or fulling cloth, and in Medieval times villagers were obliged to take their produce to be ground at the manorial mill for a charge. There were many watermills scattered through the peninsula and although a few have managed to survive, most are in ruins, including the Penrice mill which lies in the valley just north of the village. There was a mill here from at least the 16th century, but the present building dates from the 19th century and fell into disuse in the 1890's. The curious wheel-shaped pit nearby is probably a fish-stew built in the 18th century to provide Penrice Castle with a ready supply of fish.

Penrice church.

The outer face of Penrice castle gatehouse.

Penrice Castle (30). There are in fact, three 'castles' at Penrice and one of them, Mounty Bank ringwork, has already been mentioned; the others are an 18th century mansion and a very substantial 13th century stone fortress.

The Penres or Penrhys family are recorded in Gower from the early 12th century, and in all probability they were among the first Norman settlers to arrive in the wake of Henry de Beaumont's invasion in 1106. The earth and timber defences of Mounty Bank served their needs until the early 13th century when Robert de Penres decided to relocate to a new site about half a mile away to the north. Steep natural slopes and cliffs provided adequate defence on most sides, and on the weaker landward flank he built a two storied round keep (a very modest version of the towers then appearing in the Welsh Marches). There was an adjoining defensive wall, but only a few fragments of this now survive and the precise layout is unclear.

Most of the existing stonework was built late in the 13th century either in response to the growing power of Prince Llywelyn ap Gruffudd, or as a precaution after the downfall of the Welsh ruler. The work may have been carried out by William de Penres who, in 1284, was granted a respite from knighthood by King Edward I, perhaps as a concession to the financial burden of castle building. Certainly Penrice would have been an expensive edifice for a relatively minor family to construct, for it is the largest of the Gower castles comprising an area of about an acre, enclosed by high walls studded with turrets. Yet despite its size the castle is very basic and lacks

Cutaway reconstruction of the gatehouse, Penrice Castle.

the fine dressed stonework we see in Oystermouth or Swansea; perhaps the finer details were reserved for the hall block which lay between the keep and gatehouse and has been largely demolished. This destruction is believed to have been the result of Roundhead cannonfire in the Civil War, but it is far from certain that Penrice ever played a part in the conflict. What remains shows the hall to have been a large and strong two-storeyed rectangular block, with square towers at either end.

The most ambitious feature of Penrice castle is the form of the gatehouse, which is a variation on the usual theme of two towers astride the entrance passage (as at Pennard). Here there are three; two in front of the gate, and another spanning the passage at the rear. The upper floors were small and basic living chambers which were later fitted out as dovecots when the castle fell into decay. Accommodation for pigeons had already been provided by a large beehive-shaped dovecot, built against the outer wall sometime in the later Middle Ages.

The castle remained with the Penres family until the early 15th century, when the heiress, Isabel, married into the Mansels of Oxwich. Presumably it was still occupied until about the middle of the 16th century when Sir Rice Mansel leased it out. The domestic accommodation was then transferred to a farmhouse lower down the hill, but in the 18th century the property passed to a minor branch of the Mansels and work began on a new mansion in 1773. This was designed by the architect Anthony Keck and largely finished by 1777, though the landscaped gardens, lilyponds, and ornamental walks took a further 17 years to complete. The old fortress was not completely abandoned in this civilized period; a large brick building was constructed in the courtyard and some of the battlements were repaired, so that the wealthy inhabitants of 'new' Penrice Castle could stroll along the ivy-covered walls and oversee their fine estate.

Neither the house nor the castle is open to the public, although they can be veiwed from a public footpath which crosses the grounds, starting from the gates opposite the old mill and ending near a lay-by on the A4118.

Reynoldston (31) lies on the edge of the great common of Cefn Bryn, just off the A4118 about half a mile east of the Penrice turn. The village is believed to be named after the founder, Reginald de Breos (d1221), but today there are few signs of its Medieval origin, and even the parish church was rebuilt in the last century. All that survives of the earlier building is the font, and a round-headed window reset in the chancel wall. The church does contain an Early Christian stone monument which formerly stood in a field to the south (where it is still marked on OS maps). The tall narrow slab has been carved with two crosses and a Celtic knotwork design, and was probably the gravestone of a ninth-century dignitary. Sadly, years of exposure to the elements have worn away much of the elaborate pattern.

In a field behind the King Arthur Inn is a ploughed-down bank and ditch enclosure of probable Iron Age date, although there is some speculation that it may have been the Medieval home of the Lucas family before they moved to nearby Stouthall in the 15th century.

Cefn Bryn

From Reynoldston village centre a signposted road to Llanrhidian climbs the side of Cefn Bryn, a long limestone ridge aptly described as the 'backbone of Gower'. The summit trackway and the numerous paths which fan out across the lower slopes provide easy access to the numerous Prehistoric sites scattered about the gorse and bracken covered common. The hill can be reached by several signposted paths off the A4118 between Reynoldston and Penmaen Green, but the car park on the highest point of the Llanrhidian road is an ideal starting point and central base for exploration.

Along the eastern part of the ridge between the car park and Penmaen, there are about 15 Bronze Age burial mounds; those along the summit track are fairly easy to locate, but the others on the gentler north-facing slopes take a bit of tracking down. One group located about half-way along the ridge on the north side (at grid reference SS 503 896) include three ring cairns, one with the tumbled remains of large kerbstones.

Nicholaston Long Cairn (32).
On the south side of the hill, between the hamlets of Perriswood and Parsonage Farm, are the remains of a small Neolithic tomb. It lies just uphill of the boundary wall marking the edge of common land, and was discovered during quarrying work in 1939. The most prominent feature of the site today is the central burial chamber, a slab-lined grave roofed over with two flat stones in the middle of a poorly-preserved oval mound. The chamber is much smaller than most Neolithic tombs and is more reminiscent of Bronze Age burial cists (like the one on Llanmadoc Hill). No human remains were found inside since the chamber had been broken into in the past. Furthermore, no evidence came to light of a passage connecting the chamber with the edge of the mound, and it is possible that the tomb was constructed for a single occasion, rather than the more usual practice of communal burial where the entrance would be sealed after each inhumation.

Walterston deserted Medieval village (33)
Directly north of the Nicholaston cairn, on the opposite side of Cefn Bryn, can be found the most complete deserted village site on Gower. At Pennard, Penmaen and Rhossili only parts of the settlement have been excavated and recorded, here at Walterston the lost hamlet survives as stony earthworks fossilized into the landscape. The site lies in the fields west of Great

A conjectural reconstruction of the deserted village at Walterston.

Walterston farm on the very edge of the common. A footpath running along the outside of the 19th century field wall may have been the village street at one time, and the foundations of six stone houses can be seen on the other side of the wall. Less easy to spot are the low banks which enclosed a series of long and narrow boundary plots behind the houses.

The 'villa walter' was in existence by the end of the 12th century, and the settlement also included a chapel (which has yet to be located). Around 1220 the property passed into the ownership of Neath Abbey, and the monks established a grange (farm) here to work the land. The little village survived the seizure and sale of monastic property at the Reformation, and lingered on into the 19th century. Three buildings are shown here on the Llanrhidian tithe map of 1848, but by the time of the 1877 OS map they had crumbled into the ground.

Arthur's Stone (34)

Back at the car park on the Reynoldston-Llanrhidian road there is a well-marked footpath which leads north over the brow of Cefn Bryn to the most famous Prehistoric monument on the peninsula, Arthur's Stone, or Maen Ceti. This Neolithic burial chamber was one of the first sites to be protected under the Ancient Monuments Act of 1882, and it is not hard to see why; the capstone covering the burial chamber is an immense boulder of mill-stone grit estimated to weigh at least 30 tons. Many legends are connected with the site; that it was a pebble King Arthur found in his shoe, the cap-stone rolls down to the Burry stream for a drink on Midsummer eve, there are sacred wells bubbling up underneath it. These stories, and more, have nothing to do with the reasons the tomb was originally constructed, but simply reflect the way in which the ancient relic has impressed itself on the imagination of Gower locals.

The massive capstone was probably not placed here by the brute efforts of Stone Age workmen, but by the immensely slower action of a glacier in the last Ice Age. What the tomb builders did was to excavate a cavity under the stone and prop it up with slabs, forming two low burial compartments underneath. The circular pit was then filled in with a cairn of loose stones, though it is unlikely that the huge capstone was ever covered over completely. A visitor to Cefn Bryn 5,000 years ago would have seen a low mound of rocks and boulders with the upthrusting mass of the capstone rising from the centre.

In the Bronze Age the area around Arthur's Stone was again used for funerary rites and burials. Over sixty cairns can be found in a relatively small area east and west of the tomb, and while some are likely to be genuine burial sites, many of the mounds could be nothing more than heaps of stones cleared off the land for agricultural use. Two sites here have been classed as 'ritual rings', one lies about 300m south-east of the tomb, and could be the remains of a ring cairn; the other can be found in the undergrowth 150m to the north-east and consists of a long low mound inside a ring ditch about 30m across.

Arthur's Stone: the massive capstone covers two small burial chambers underneath.

Alongside a faint path which leads east from Arthur's Stone is a group of about half a dozen boulders spaced about 100m apart, and in a rough east west alignment. In the last century this was believed to be a rare stone avenue, a type of Bronze Age ritual monument more often encountered in Cornwall and Devon; but there are so many natural rocks scattered about the hill that the apparent alignment could be a natural formation.

More prominent, and of proven antiquity, are three cairns located north and west of Arthur's Stone and which were excavated between 1981 and 1984. The largest is Great Carn, a saucer-shaped mound of stones raised over a central grave pit. Excavation also revealed that there was earlier activity at the site, long before the cairn was built, in the form of a late Neolithic settlement. On the slopes to the north are two ring cairns, the larger having a single entrance gap and an inner ring of kerb stones. The spcae within the enclosure bank was filled in with stones at a later date, either as part of a ritual, or to end any ceremonies taking place there.

Returning now through Reynoldston to the main coast road, and the A4118 soon passes the landscaped grounds of Stouthall mansion, home to a branch of the Lucas family. The plain classical building was completed 1790 to a plan reminiscent of Penrice Castle, and replaced a much older house which stood nearby.

Knelston (35) is the next stop along, and while the modern buildings lining the road offer little to the historian, just out of sight in the fields behind is a strange juxtaposition of Christian and pagan monuments. Just past the

Knelston standing stone.

school a right hand lane to Knelston Hall Farm is the start of a signposted public footpath to Burry. A short way along the lane and the crumbling remains of a building will be seen in a field on the right hand side. This was the Medieval village church, known as Llan y Tair Mair, the church of the three Marys. The ruin is now in a sorry state; engulfed by nettles and trees, buried in rubble, and with only a single precarious fragment of masonry standing more than head-high. What can be seen of the plan suggests this was a simple rectangular building divided into a chancel and nave, possibly with a south porch. There is some evidence that the chancel is a later addition, and so the church may originally have been a single cell building like Caswell.

Knelston church remained in use well after the Reformation but, like Trinity Well at Ilston, appears to have fallen foul of the zealous Puritans in the 17th century. According to Isaac Hamon there was 'in the time of King Charles I a pretty church, but it hath been eversince open and uncovered and nothing done there but burialles'.

Beyond the last of the farm buildings, just a field away from the church, is an even older monument connected to the long-lost beliefs and ceremonies of Prehistoric Man. This 2.2m high slab of millstone grit is one of the best examples of a Bronze Age standing stone in Gower. Though it is not the tallest – that prize goes to Carreg Bica (81) – it is perhaps the most impressive since it has not been incorporated into a hedgerow like so many other sites. The proximity of Christian and Prehistoric sites has already been mentioned, and the building of the church here may have been an attempt to sanctify a well-known pagan area. There are two more stones about 1km further along the path in the direction of Burry. They lie on either side of the same field close to the hedgerows, although one has fallen. The other stands 1.6m high, and an 18th century estate map shows two adjoining stones which have since been removed. Evidently the Knelston-Burry area was of some importance to the Bronze Age tribes of Gower.

Llanddewi (36).

If Knelston village thrived at the expense of its church, then the opposite must be true of Llanddewi, for the parish church of St David stands alone and aloof, with only a single farm to keep it company. Even the road planners appear to have encouraged this rural isolation; the A4118 makes a beeline for Llanddewi and then abruptly changes course for Port Eynon. A short detour along a lane is necessary to reach the place.

Despite extensive restoration work enough original features remain to enable the development of the church to be traced fairly easily. A single round-headed window in the north wall indicates that the nave was built in the 12th century, and the Norman church may have been of no greater extent than this; just a single room building like Caswell. Late in the 12th, or early in the 13th century, the chancel was built out from the east wall at a rather curious angle. The west tower may also date from the same period since the low and slightly pointed entrance arch is similar to the chancel

Llanddewi church.

arch, but the saddleback roof is a later modification. The porch, nave door, and some windows were added as part of a general refurbishment in the 14th century. The timber roof is modern.

Across the yard from the church is *Llanddewi Castle*, a modern-looking building with rendered walls and a tiled roof; but appearances are very often deceptive, and beneath the nondescript facade there is a substantial house dating back to the 16th century. The building has a T-shaped plan comprising a hall and kitchen blocks with a large stair tower jutting out from one side. The stair has solid oak treads rising around a central stone pillar and this type of feature, known as a 'pillar stair', is usually found in large upper-class houses, like Oxwich Castle. The 'lateral' fireplace in the side wall of the hall is another feature denoting a high status. The present

Reconstruction drawing of Llanddewi Castle as it may have looked, c.1600.

owners have recently begun stripping the old rendering from the walls, revealing some hidden features including a large blocked window which must have illuminated the first floor hall.

But the story of Llanddewi Castle goes further back than Elizabethan times, as the place-name suggests. Llanddewi was a residence of the Bishops of St David's and that enthusiastic builder, Henry de Gower, is reported to have constructed a sumptuous 'palace' here. However, mounting expenses forced the clergy to make financial cutbacks, and the remote location and poor water supply made Llanddewi a casualty. The palace is said to have been dismantled by Henry's successor, Bishop Houghton, but part of the structure must surely be incorporated into the existing house, for the walls in places are almost 2m thick.

This is not the only vanished castle in Gower; documentary evidence exists for what were probably fortified residences at Port Eynon, Henllys, and Scurlage. The latter stood only 1km away beside the road to Port

Eynon, a site now occupied by a modern farm. It was built in the 14th century by the Scurlage family, and later passed to the Mansels of Oxwich.

PORT EYNON, RHOSSILI, AND THE SOUTH COAST

The coastal scenery between Rhossili and Port Eynon is arguably the finest in all the peninsula, with a succession of sheer limestone cliffs and rocky valleys culminating in the sinuous rock of Worms Head. Geology and the elements have conspired to create a dramatic landscape which is not only admired by present-day visitors, but once attracted the attention of far earlier inhabitants of this land. Large areas of the coastline are owned by the National Trust and there are several waymarked footpaths leading along the cliffs to Rhossili, starting from Port Eynon village, Overton, or from the B4247 at Pilton Green.

In the village a few 18th-century whitewashed cottages survive, though sadly no longer thatched, along with the parish church of St Catwg which was restored and enlarged in 1861 and 1901. The chancel originally had a round arch indicating a 12th century origin, with a north transept and south porch added at a much later date. The most curious feature of Port Eynon church is the absence of an east window above the altar.

The Salt House (37)
From the car park on Port Eynon foreshore a path leads through the burrows on the western side of the bay, to a ruined building on the very edge of the sea. So many legends and half-truths have gathered around the Salt House that it comes almost as a suprise to find out it was (as the name implies) a factory producing salt from seawater. This is believed to be the earliest saltworks in Wales and is the only one to survive in Gower. Isaac Hamon referred to salt houses at Oystermouth and Kilvey, and on Emmanuel Bowen's map of South Wales (1729) another is shown at Cheriton; but these have vanished except for the place-names, and the same fate was thought to have befallen this site until the Glamorgan-Gwent Archaeological Trust began excavating here in 1986. The resultant discoveries proved to be so important that a strong wall was built around the site to protect it from any further coastal erosion.

According to the traditional stories, the house was built around 1500 by David Lucas as a wedding present to his wayward son John. David hoped he would settle down, but John had other ideas and set about 'making a stronghold of ye Salte House, with the battlement and walls whereof all round, reaching even unto the cliff'. Using his house as a base, John pursued a lucrative career as a smuggler and wrecker. A descendant (another John) died in the house during a terrible storm in the early 18th century and 'in the same dreadful night a bolt did come upon ye Salte House ...

A view of the excavated buildings at the Salt House.

and ye sea broke ye battlements thereof and tore it even unto ye great Cliff and so was not to be lived in more'.

These colourful legends should be taken with a pinch of salt, yet the excavators discovered that some of the window openings had been adapted for the use of guns, so there may be a grain of truth in the tales. Salt was an important and valuable commodity and the owner may have taken precautions to protect his stock. On the beach below the house the Trust excavated a series of rectangular pits or reservoirs, which would have been filled at high tide and the water then pumped up into drying pans at a higher level. The shallow pans were then heated causing salt crystals to form from the evaporating brine.

A short distance past the ruins the coast path crosses the edge of Port Eynon Point. In the seaward facing cliff there is a large cave entrance which narrows to form a dry upper chamber, where Ice Age animal bones were found in the 1920's and '30's. A more famous cave awaits the visitor further around the headland.

Culver Hole (38)

Aptly described by the late Wynford Vaughan-Thomas as the 'great Gower mystery', this bizzare structure has puzzled visitors for years. A tall and

The entrance to the enigmatic Culver Hole.

narrow sea cave at the end of a gulley has been completely sealed up with a massive wall, pierced with openings of various shapes all connected on the inside by a flight of stone steps. At low tide it is possible to scramble up to the lower opening and climb the slippery stair.

The most popular theory concerning the origin of Culver Hole is that it was a smuggler's den or pirate stronghold; the Lucas legends recount how John 'rebuilded and repaired another stronghold called Kulverd Hall near thereunto in the rocks' and connected it to the Salt House by 'a passage under the ground'. Gripping stuff, but in fact Culver Hole was a gigantic dovecot, and the many nesting holes on the inner walls show that it was intended from the start to house pigeons, regardless of its later uses. More orthodox dovecots survive at Oxwich and Penrice castles, and testify to the widespread use of pigeons as a source of fresh meat and eggs for the aristocracy. It may be that the cave belonged to the documented (but vanished) castle of Port Eynon, which possibly stood nearby. A record dated 1428 mentions a ruined 'dovecote in the clyve' at Pennard. If this is not a mistaken reference to Culver Hole, then it might suggest that there were more of these strange buildings in the past.

The rugged escarpment west of Culver Hole provided the nomadic hunters of the Old Stone Age with refuges and temporary campsites. The

Interior view of Goat's Hole cave, Paviland.

caves they sheltered in thousands of years ago are still here, though the landscape around them has changed beyond all recognition. The first cave reached is *Longhole* (39), which lies about 1km west of Overton hamlet, at the end of a gulley just below the level of the clifftop. Of all the bone caves in Gower Longhole is the least inspiring, lacking the spectacular coastal setting of Bacon Hole or Paviland, and there is no challenge of an adventurous scramble around a cliff to get to it. The entrance is a low arch at the base of a rock face, leading into a dark winding passage about 13m long. Nevertheless, the cave played an important role in the history of British archaeology, for the results of Colonel Wood's excavations here in 1861 proved that Man and extinct animals had lived in the same period – a concept that the excavator of nearby Paviland had failed to grasp some forty years previously. More scientific work was carried out here in 1969 and the resultant finds identified Longhole as a campsite for hunting groups between 36,000 and 28,000 BC.

A further 1.5km along the coast and you reach a junction of paths at the head of a steep gulley. The right hand path leads to the main road at Pilton Green, while in the opposite direction a rough track winds down towards the sea and the famous *Paviland Caves* (40). The two caves, Goat's Hole and Hound's Hole, lie at the base of the towering Yellowtop headland, a distinctive landmark named after the mottled covering of yellowish lichen. At low tide the caves can be reached by an easy climb down and around the foot of the cliffs, but if the tide is in, then the only access is via a more difficult climb around the west side of the gulley.

In the early years of the 19th century extinct animal bones were found in the larger cave, Goat's Hole, by two brothers from Reynoldston. Their discovery was brought to the attention of local geologist Lewis Dillwyn, and Lady Mary Cole and Miss Talbot of Penrice Castle. These enthusiastic amateurs were regular correspondents with the Rev William Buckland, first professor of geology at Oxford, and on hearing of the finds Buckland wrote 'I am impatient for further accounts, and the moment I can stir, will if possible run down to get a peep at what remains in the cave'. The learned man's 'peep' was to include digging up the floor of the cave in January 1823 and uncovering the remains of a human skeleton stained with a reddish ochre. This Buckland dubbed 'the Red Woman or Witch of Paviland'. Alongside the body were numerous ivory rods and rings, a mammoth skull, and some flint tools. At that time scholarly opinion could not accept the evidence that extinct animals and man had lived at the same time, and Buckland inevitably concluded that the burial was an intrusive feature of the cave, connected with the Iron Age fort on the cliffs above. He also found it hard to believe why anyone would want to live in such an inaccessible spot; but we now know that there was no such thing as the Bristol Channel when Paviland was home to Palaeolithic man.

Buckland's dig was fairly methodical for the period, and his identification of the skeleton as a woman was based largely on the presence of the ivory 'jewellery'. For over eighty years no one challenged his opinions. The publication of Darwin's work proved that the origins of Mankind lay much further back in the past than conventional biblical views allowed, and so the 'Red Lady' (as 'she' is more widely known) was eventually recognised to be far older than the Iron Age. More meticulous excavations by Prof. W. J. Sollas (who also held Buckland's position at Oxford) brought to light over 5,000 flint artifacts from the remaining deposits in the cave, identifying Paviland as one of the richest and most important Upper Palaeolithic sites in Britain.

At intervals during a vast period of some 11,000 years, Goat's Hole was used as a base camp by groups of nomadic tribes hunting animals such as mammoth, woolly rhino and reindeer on the great plains now lost beneath the sea. Nearby Longhole and Cathole were also used as transit camps during hunting expeditions. The bones of their prey have been found in the caves, though some would have been brought in by wolves and hyenas after the hunters had moved on. The so-called Red Lady was, in fact, a man of about 25 years old, young to us, but probably middle-aged by Palaeolithic standards. For some time, archaeologists believed he had died around 16,500 BC, but more recently that date has been revised to nearer 24,000 BC. His body was laid in a shallow grave along with the ivory artifacts as votive offerings, and then dusted with red iron oxide, perhaps to simulate life giving blood.

For a period of about 15,000 years, the harsh climate made Britain uninhabitable, but from around 10,000 BC the ice was retreating and the hunters returned once more. Paviland was reoccupied, but the number of finds from this period was significantly smaller, and it has been suggested that both Paviland and Cathole were just temporary campsites used by a group based in the Mendip hills. Although the main period of settlement was over, the excavations produced finds indicating that Goat's Hole offered refuge for people in the Mesolithic, Neolithic and Roman Periods. The smaller of the two caves here, Hound's Hole, was also excavated in the last century but the finds were dissappointingly few. Most of the deposits were probably washed away by the rising tide, though 'cold period' animal bones and two Roman coins have been found.

Apart from Palaeolithic hunters these cliffs have been home to Iron Age farmers, and the remains of five defended settlements can be reached from the coast path between Paviland and Rhossili. Each site differs in size and layout and reveal the way in which the builders adapted the natural topography of the cliffs to their best defensive advantage.

Directly above the caves the narrow approach to the summit of *Yellowtop* (41) is barred by a series of widely-spaced banks and ditches, something of a defensive overkill in fact, since the ramparts cover an area twice the size of the occupational area. A short distance away to the west on the neighbouring *Horse Cliff* (42) headland, the settlers eschewed large-scale defences for a single drystone rampart with a shallow outer ditch. The cliffs provided effective protection on most sides, and the entrance was a simple gap between one end of the rampart and a sheer drop to the sea.

A reconstruction of Horse Cliff fort.

Look north from Horse Cliff to the far side of a small bay where, if the light is right, a small dark opening can be seen about half way down the rocky slope. This is the entrance to a small cave system known as *Deborah's Hole* (43) where, in 1861 Col. Wood dug up animal bones and a flint tool, possibly of Upper Palaeolithic Date.

The Knave (44) promontory fort lies on the headland of that name at the western edge of the same bay. The settlement was defended by two widely-spaced lines of banks and ditches curving around to enclose an inner area

An aerial view of The Knave promontory fort, seen from the north. (© Copyright reserved: National Monument Record for Wales).

of about 0.1ha. The ramparts are today overgrown and reduced in size by erosion and stone robbing, but they were originally formidable barriers of thick rubble banks faced with drystone walls. The outermost entrance is a simple gap through the bank, but excavations in 1938 revealed a line of three post holes in the passageway, suggesting there were two wooden gates (hung on side posts) which closed on a central pole. The inner entrance did not have a wooden gate, but was protected by an inturned rampart (so that an enemy entering the enclosure would have been exposed to attack from the side). Traces of a wattle and daub roundhut were discovered in the angle of the bank, and from its position and comparison with other Iron Age sites, it was very probably a guardroom. A second hut was located near the cliff edge; this had been burned down, but whether by accident or an enemy attack is impossible to say. Among the finds from the 1938 excavation were pieces of Iron Age pottery dating from around 50BC to AD50, similar to pottery samples from Glastonbury in Somerset. Were the occupants of The Knave fort settlers from the west country, bringing with them their valuable utensils, or were they just bought by a local family from the Iron Age equivalent of a travelling salesman?

From The Knave there is a walk of about 1.5km along the undulating clifftop to the next fort, situated on the rugged outcrop of *Thurba Head* (45). Although the rock is naturally strong it is far from level, being broken by outcrops and slopes, and the builders took advantage of the lie of the land to channel the direction of any attack along a narrow shelf below the ramparts. An enemy succeeding in avoiding missiles hurled by the defenders above would then be faced with the daunting prospect of an uphill climb to the entrance. It is possible that the small inner enclosure was the first fort here, the more extensive outer ramparts being added at a later date.

Beyond Thurba Head the path dips down into Mew Slade and merges with another path leading from the beach to the main Rhossili road at Pitton. There is another small fort at *Lewes Castle* (46) overlooking Fall Bay on the far side of Mew Slade, and the path that skirts the double bank and ditch enclosure can be followed around to Worm's Head and Rhossili. An alternative route is to continue inland along the slade, passing close to a small cave (47) where Mesolithic flint tools were discovered around 1914. In the last century Col. Wood made an important discovery in another cave, the remains of six or seven human skeletons associated with extinct animal bones, conceivably of Upper Palaeolithic date. Unfortunately, there is much uncertainty about the circumstances of the excavation, and the finds have not been located. Even the cave itself is not known, though it may have lain in a small quarry on the left of the path, near the top of the valley.

Rhossili (48)

Rhossili is the westernmost village in Gower, a quiet outpost of cottages and houses lining the road that snakes past the parish church of St. Mary. To the north-east the village is overlooked by the bleak ridge of Rhossili

Rhossili church.

Down, while northwards stretches the great expanse of Rhossili Bay, the graveyard of many ships. The village lies on the clifftop overlooking the bay, but the original Medieval settlement was established in the burrows close to the beach. During the winter of 1979-80 storm water eroded the topsoil, exposing bones and fragments of masonry, and a team from the Glamorgan-Gwent Archaeological Trust began excavating the affected areas. They found the remains of several houses and exposed the foundation walls of a large building, oblong in plan but with rounded corners like the halls at Pennard and Penmaen. Not far away to the north-east the archaeologists investigated a large stony mound which turned out to be the buried remains of the old church. The chancel and part of the nave were uncovered, revealing plain, unglazed windows and, more importantly, the remains of painted designs and inscriptions on the walls. Such mural decorations rarely survive today, yet they can lurk undetected beneath layers of whitewash and plaster.

The history of old Rhossili is now lost to us. There is a possibility that the church was founded as an Early Christian centre, and its demise can perhaps be blamed on the sand incursions which finished off the villages at Pennard and Penmaen. Some of the excavated walls can still be seen alongside the steep path leading down to the beach.

The existing church of St Mary is no older than the beginning of the 14th century and its construction probably indicates the time at which the old settlement was abandoned. It is possible that the two churches were in use together, but there is one feature which suggests that the death of old Rhossili signalled the birth of the new. The main entrance to the church is through a splendid late Norman doorway, which is well over a century older than the rest of the fabric, and has clearly been re-set in its present place. One or more of the stones were lost in the process, giving the arch a slightly lop-sided look. Tradition, backed up by archaeological evidence, claims that this was the chancel archway of the old church. The plain round-headed doorway is framed by a deeply incised chevron arch supported on pillars, with an outer arch of dog-tooth carvings terminating in grotesque heads. There is a third head near the top of the arch. On the left hand pillar can be seen a rare 'scratch dial', a simple form of sundial where the hours were read by the shadow of a pointer inserted into the central hole. The porch is a modern addition.

There is an original 14th century window in the south wall of the chancel which, from its low position, is known as a 'leper's window' and was supposedly used by those feared outcasts of Medieval society to hear mass without entering the building. Rhossili church also had a fine saddleback tower, the only one in Gower without a masking parapet or battlements. In the summer of 1994 part of the nave wall was stripped of plaster revealing the line of a raised roof and a blocked gable window, which indicates that the tower is an addition. Apart from the door and chancel window the church has few other surviving early features thanks to over-zealous Victorian restoration work. The most notable monument here is a plaque commemorating Petty Officer Edgar Evans, a native of the parish, who accompanied Captain Scott on the ill-fated expedition to the Antarctic in 1912.

From the village car park a well-marked footpath leads to the westernmost point of Gower, passing on the left an area of 'open' fields. This rare survival of Medieval agricultural practices consists of a patchwork of long, narrow fields, most separated only by a thin strip of uncultivated ground. Other field systems remain in the vicinity of Bishopston, Murton and Llanmadoc, but here the arable strips are largely unaltered or enclosed by later hedges.

To the right of the path on a broad gorse covered headland is the site of *Old Castle camp* (49), a bank and ditch enclosure of probable Iron Age date. The place-name and semi-circular plan have given rise to the suggestion that it may have been a Norman ringwork built to defend the early settlement; but the ramparts are far too slight compared to genuine Medieval ringworks, and the camp is too far from Rhossili to be of any immediate use. Despite the undergrowth and damage caused by quarrying the curving defensive line can be made out, with a possible entrance gap on the southwest side.

Worms Head (50)
About 1 km beyond Old Castle the footpath reaches the channel separating the mainland from the sinuous rock of Worms Head. For a few hours either side of low tide it is possible to cross a natural causeway to the headland, but check in advance at Rhossili about the tide times; Worms Head can be an inhospitable place to be trapped for half a day waiting for the right tide! In the last century a rock arch and a natural blow-hole were popular tourist attractions here, some people even sailing through the arch by boat. An even earlier traveller, Henry VIII's official antiquarian, John Leland, was more interested in another cave on the rock; 'There is also a wonderfull Hole at the poyant of Worme Heade, but few dare entre into it, and Men fable there that a Dore within the spatius Hole hathe be sene withe great Nayles on it'. Leland's archaic text also mentions an underground passage connecting Worms Head with caves near Llandybïe and Carreg Cennen castle in Carmarthenshire. Despite the fact that anyone can disprove this story, the tradition of caves and secret tunnels linking far-flung places is widespread and enduring. Leland's cave can be found on a sloping rock ledge at the most westerly tip of the headland, but the only access is via an awkward climb around the cliff base. The entrance is the uppermost of two small caves, and it leads into a dark chamber with a short passage at the rear. Two excavations carried out here in the first quarter of this century produced finds of uncertain Prehistoric date, including human and animal bones, flint flakes and a sling-stone.

Despite the present-day access problems (caused by centuries of coastal erosion) this windswept headland was inhabited at other periods in the past. There is a small Iron Age fort on the inner 'hump' of the Worm, and around 1910 a stone mould for casting metal ornaments was discovered here. On the gentler slopes beneath the fort are several ruined stone buildings which may be sheepfolds or cottages. There is a story that one of the buildings had a false cellar where smuggled liquor was hidden during the Napoleonic Wars!

Rhossili Down (51)
Behind the village the gorse and bracken covered slopes of Rhossili Down rise to a height of 193m above sea level, providing a dramatic backdrop to the sandy sweep of the bay. There is a waymarked path starting from the church which leads to the summit and then on down into Llangennith village. A longer, but less steep, route to the same destination can be taken along the beach, past Burry Holms, and across Llangennith Burrows.

Today Rhossili Down attracts ramblers, pony trekkers and hang gliding enthusiasts, but between 3 and 4 thousand years ago the ridge was a sacred burial site for the Bronze Age hierarchy of Gower. Around a dozen cairns lie dotted along the ridge and the gentler eastern slopes. Most are the usual round type, but there are one or two rings, and a very good platform cairn with a prominent kerb of stones, located about 300m north of the OS pillar on the summit.

The best preserved of the Sweyne's Howes burial chambers.

By the time the Bronze Age tribes were piling stones over graves, the hill had already done service as a cemetary. Further along the ridge are the remains of two Neolithic tombs, known as *Sweyne's Howes* (52), a name which recalls the eponymous founder of Swansea, the Viking Sweyne. In reality these burial chambers have nothing whatsoever to do with Norsemen, and there is a possibility that the name actually derives from 'the swine's houses', a reference to the hut-like appearance of the tombs. Today, though, the chambers are badly ruined, particularly the southern one which is an almost indistinguishable jumble of stones with an oval surrounding cairn robbed almost to ground level. A few upright slabs look like the remains of a ceremonial facade at the entrance to the tomb, similar to the more complete monument at Pentre Ifan in Pembrokshire. The north chamber is better preserved and two out of three uprights partly support the fallen capstone.

Burry Holms (53)
Burry Holms is the little tidal island at the furthest point of Rhossili Bay, a grassy rock barely 400m long and rising no more than 30m above the sea, and yet it encapsulates in miniature almost the entire history of the Gower peninsula, a history which started around 8000 years ago. At a time when the island was just a low ridge overlooking plains and forests, Mesolithic hunters camped here and lost some of their distinctive stone tools which

were found again by modern archaeologists. In the Bronze Age when the sea level had risen and probably lapped at the foot of the rock, a chieftain was buried under a round cairn on the summit. A few centuries later, Iron Age settlers fortified part of the headland by digging a bank and ditch from one side to the other, barring access to any intruder.

The most important phase of the island's history came in the centuries after the collapse of the Roman Empire, when Christianity was slowly spreading through the land. 'Holms' is a Norse word for island, and this not only suggests that the vikings were familiar with the Gower coastline, but also that by the Dark Ages the sea had cut through the ridge leaving it as it is today, accessible only at low tide. The lure of a remote and relatively inaccessible site appealed to Early Christian hermits and holy men, and St Cenydd, the founder of Llangennith, is believed to have established an oratory here in the 6th century. Indeed, it is possible that Burry Holms was the site of Cenydd's original foundation, before it was relocated to a more convenient inland site at Llangennith.

Between 1965 and 1968 the Royal Commission on Ancient & Historical Monuments carried out a series of excavations on the ruined buildings still visible on the more sheltered east side of the island. Archaeologists discovered the buried foundations of a turf and stone boundary wall enclosing an oval graveyard, with a timber round hut outside. A small square wooden chapel or oratory was later built inside the enclosure, and this may have been the work of Caradoc of Rhos who re-established the shrine of St Cenydd in the late 11th century.

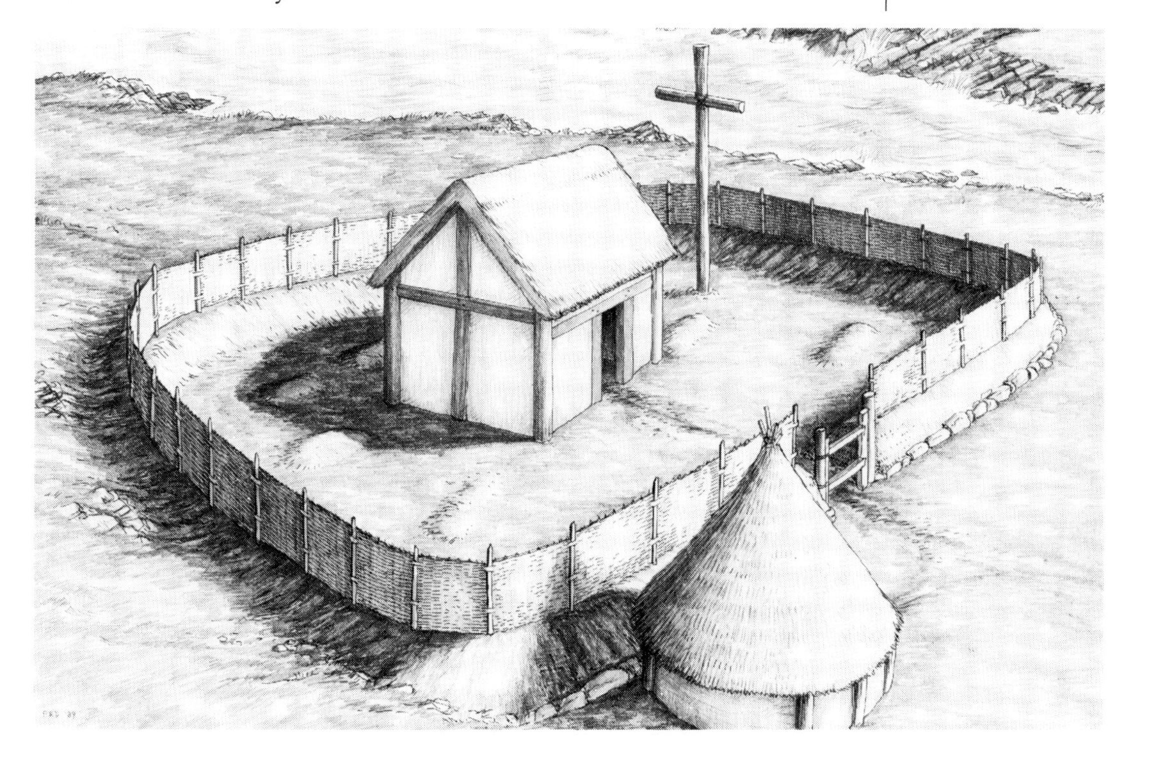

Burry Holms: a conjectural reconstruction of the pre-Norman timber church and enclosure.

Burry Holms: the ruins of the 12th century church in the foreground, with the foundations of the hall to the right.

Following the Norman invasion of Gower this simple structure was replaced by a slightly larger stone building with the rare feature of an apsidal (round-ended) chancel. There were contemporary dwellings on the south side, but the grass-covered foundations now visible are the remains of a later domestic hall with an adjoining cloister-like courtyard. The settlement reached its greatest extent in the 14th century, when a school or assembly room was built on the north side of the church. This had internal rows of tiered stone seats and an entrance porch. The apse was also replaced by a more conventional rectangular chancel. There is a document of 1398 which records a royal grant of 'the hermitage of St Kenyth atte Holmes in Gowerslond' to a hermit named Philip Lichepoll; similar grants are also recorded in the 15th century. The fate of the ecclesiastical complex on Burry Holms is not recorded, but in all probability the Reformation brought to an end any pilgrimages to the island and the income necessary for the upkeep of the buildings.

Less than 2km east of the island, the craggy cliffs and secluded bays give way to a different landscape of sand warrens and salt marshes. As if giving a final flourish the sculpting force of the sea has created the well known Three Chimneys and the tidal pond at Bluepool Corner, but less familiar is the mysterious *Culver Hole* (54). Access is only possible at low tide by climbing over the Three Chimneys headland, and then sqeezing through a narrow vertical fissure in the cliff. Very little light enters the boulder strewn chamber and so a torch is really needed for exploration. Some human bones were found in the cave in the late 19th century, but more detailed excavations carried out in the 1920's and 30's yielded the remains of at least forty skeletons, objects of bone and flint, and fragments of about a dozen clay funerary urns. These urns are of late Bronze Age date and the skeletons too may be contemporary. However, the archaeological deposits had been disturbed by the encroaching sea, and there is a possibility that the burials could be of Iron Age or Roman date. A number of artifacts of this period were recovered, including coins, brooches and pottery, as well as a metal brooch of the 9th century AD. The absence of any hearth, coupled with the difficult access and risk of flooding, strongly suggests that Culver Hole was never a home for the living, just a dark, echoing, tomb.

LLANGENNITH TO LOUGHOR: THE NORTH COAST OF GOWER

Llangennith (55) nestles in the gap between Llanmadoc Hill and Rhossili Down, sheltered from the prevailing winds but with open views westwards across the burrows to Pembrokeshire. From Burry Holms it is only a walk of a few kilometres across the burrows and along quiet lanes to reach the village, but if touring Gower by car then the only access by road is either along the B4295 via Llanrhidian, or the Burry Green road from Reynoldston.

The village is dominated by the parish church of St Cenydd, which is the largest in Gower and the only one to have had a monastic status. Though the existing building dates from the early 14th century the origins of the church lie in the murky period of history known as the Dark Ages. According to a legend set down in Tudor times, the first church was established in

Llangennith church.

Llangennith church: the impressive 'Dolly Mare' tomb effigy.

the 6th century AD by St Cenydd, the crippled offspring of an adulterous union. The far-from-holy circumstances of his conception forced Cenydd's parents to try and hide their guilty secret, and the baby was set adrift in a wicker basket on the Loughor estuary. The little boat drifted around the coast and fetched up on 'Ynysweryn' – possibly Worms Head or Burry Holms – where the child was cared for by wild animals. One day an angel told the young man of his mission in life, and he left to establish a shrine on the mainland. Scenes from the life of St Cenydd are depicted on the modern churchyard gates.

That imaginative story probably contains a grain of truth, and the link between Burry Holms and Llangennith remained throughout the Middle Ages, recalling other dual ecclesiastical sites such as Bardsey-Aberdaron and Priestholm-Penmon in north Wales. According to one chronicle the bangor or college that grew up around the shrine was pillaged by the Vikings in the 10th century. Some historians have doubted whether this event took place, but the presence of Norsemen in Gower is attested not only by place-name evidence but also the discovery of finds of the period (such as the Minchin Hole coins and the Culver Hole brooch).

In the years between 1066 and the Norman invasion of Gower, the Pembrokeshire holy man Caradoc of Rhos, travelled to Llangennith and restored the neglected and overgrown shrine. Bishop Herewald of Llandaf ordained Caradoc as 'a monk in lann Cinith', though he later moved back to Haverfordwest, where he died in 1124. Many miracles are attributed to Caradoc; and the famous writer and traveller, Gerald of Wales, even tried to get his fellow countryman enrolled among the official saints. By the time of Caradoc's death Henry de Beaumont had already laid claim to Gower and, in the fashion of other Norman lords, he granted the property of the Welsh church to the Benedictine Abbey of St Taurin in Evreux, France. The Earl's gift comprised 'the church of St Kenetus and land for two ploughs ... a suitable spot for a mill ... and the churches of Taurin (Knelston?) Pennart (Pennard) with the tithes, and the church of the isle (Burry Holms)'.

To capitalise on their gift the monks of St Taurin established a priory cell, but that does not mean there was a grand monastery here like Neath or Tintern, bustling with holy men and silent monks; there was only a prior in charge with one or more companions, whose job it was to oversee the running of the estate and collect the revenues for the mother church in France. Far from the watchful gaze of his superiors, the prior of Llangennith could relax a little; Gerald of Wales penned a caustic tale of one prior who was caught having an affair with a local girl! There is an unproven tradition that the farm alongside the church incorporates the remains of monastic buildings, but they would not have been of any great extent and comprised just a small house for the prior and his guests. It may be that the domestic buildings excavated on Burry Holms were also used by the prior as a sort of Medieval 'holiday home' where he could retire for solitude and contemplation. Perhaps it was on this remote island away from nosy neighbours that the amorous prior carried on his affair?

Because of its status as a foreign or 'alien' priory Llangennith suffered during the Hundred Years War with France, and its possessions were frequently seized by the Crown. This precarious existence came to an end in the reign of Henry V when the priory was suppressed, and the property was later granted to All Souls College in Oxford. Though this ended Llangennith's monastic status, the church continued to serve the needs of the parishoners as, indeed, it had done for centuries before. Most abbeys and priories allowed local people to worship in the church, and very often this saved part of the building from destruction at the Dissolution in 1536-40.

Here at Llangennith the local population greatly outnumbered the priors, and the church appears to have been wholly given over to parochial use.

Despite the scale of the building the layout is a familiar one, comprising a nave, chancel, porch and a tall saddleback tower. The position of the entrance on the north side is less usual; it may be that the south door was never used by the parishoners because it led to the prior's dwelling and was sealed off at the Dissolution. The most puzzling feature of Llangennith church is a blocked up Norman arch in the east wall of the tower, which can be seen from outside. In size and appearance it is virtually identical to the plastered over chancel arches at Oxwich, Penrice and Llanmadoc, and in all probability represents the last vestiges of the 12th century priory church. No other masonry here appears to be as old as the arch which is probably *in situ* rather than having been removed from elsewhere (as happened at Rhossili). The most plausible explanation for this feature is that around 1300 the priors decided to replace the small Norman Church, and began work on a larger building alongside. In this way the services could be continued with little disruption. When the new church was almost finished they demolished the old building except for the chancel arch, and then constructed the tower around the remaining wall. The intention may have been to use the arch as a prestigious entry to a side chapel north of the chancel (this would also explain why there are no windows on this side). If this was the plan, then the work was obviously never carried to fruition, the ambitious scheme cut short perhaps by escalating costs, or by the political troubles suffered by the priory during the Hundred Years War.

Llangennith church was extensively restored in the last century and the floor level of the nave several feet, so that two tomb recesses in the south wall are now only a few inches high. Several memorial slabs were also dug up and removed, including a weathered slab carved with intricate knot-work designs which is now fixed to the west wall. At the time it was identified as 'St Cenydd's gravestone' but in fact the slab is only a fragment of what must have been a very fine wheel-cross of 9th century date. The church has one more treasure to single out, a damaged but still impressive tomb-effigy of a knight in armour. No one knows for certain who the effigy is meant to represent, although the nickname 'Dolly Mare' suggests it was one of the De la Mares. The armour worn by the figure is a simple chain-mail suit of c.1300, much more primitive than the metal plate armour of the Oxwich 'Doolamur', and yet this sculpture has a vibrancy and life that the pious supplicatory gestures of the Oxwich figures lack. The body is twisting around on the slab as if about to get up, with the right hand drawing the sword. Part of the shield still remains, but unfortunately everything below the knees has gone; probably the crossed legs rested on a small lion or dog.

On the village green outside the church is St Cenydd's well, which was originally surrounded with large boulders and covered with a flat stone. There was a cross carved into the upper surface of the slab, suggesting it was a Dark Age memorial or, more likely, a Medieval gravestone. The

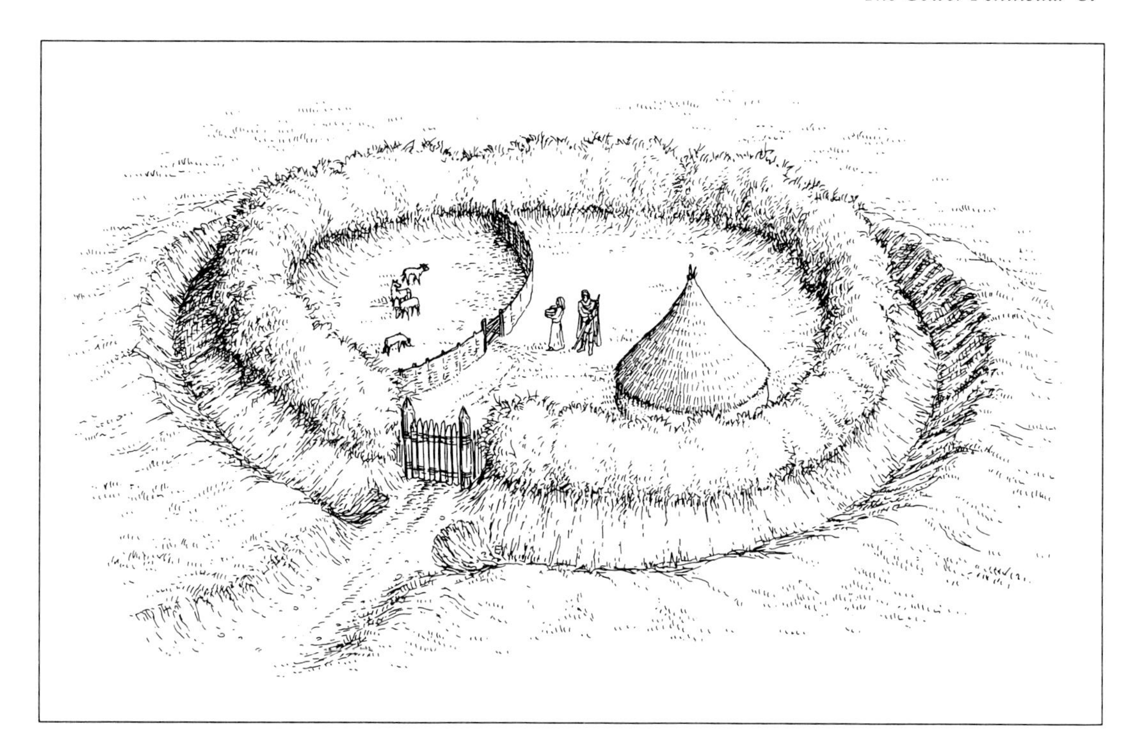

A conjectural reconstruction of Hardings Down (north) fort.

spring was sealed up in the late 19th century to prevent animals fouling th water supply, and now the cold clear waters gush out of a modern well-house. The lane beside the well curves past the church and descends to Coety Green, where the priors had their water mill. The ruined buildings dotted about the fields and woods here are the remains of a hamlet abandoned in much more recent times than those of Penmaen and Rhossili. None of the buildings appears to be earlier than the 18th century, but there is documentary evidence of an older settlement here.

Hardings Down (56)
From Coety green several paths lead over the hill to Rhossili, and eastwards up the bracken grown slopes of Hardings Down. Although this is the smallest of the three hills at the end of Gower, overlooked by the bleaker heights of Llanmadoc Hill and Rhossili Down, it was chosen by Iron Age tribes as the location for no less than three fortified settlements. The earthwork defences of the forts are clearly visible from the main road, and present a daunting obstacle for ramblers even today, over two thousand years after they were constructed. The smallest enclosure is a bank and ditch ringwork located on the north slopes of the hill. The entrance gap is approached along a sunken trackway and there are surface indications of a single round hut inside.

On the western slopes is a larger enclosure surrounded by a rampart and ditch, with a slighter bank along the outer edge of the ditch. Two more banks and ditches defend the uphill (east) flank. There are signs of three

Restored view of Delvid Farm, showing the outshut *for a bed-cupboard.*

hut sites in the interior, and the entrance, like that at the north fort, is a simple break in the rampart. However, excavations by the Royal Commission on Ancient & Historical Monuments in 1962 revealed a cobbled road surface between four large post-holes, which would have held the vertical timbers of a gatehouse. Pottery fragments from one of the excavated huts were dated to the period 100-50BC. The third fort was never finished, but the layout of the surviving banks suggests that the entire hilltop was to be enclosed, an area of about 0.9ha.

The scarcity of huts within the two completed forts indicates that these substantial earthworks sheltered only one or two families at most, rather than a thriving community. But perhaps they were only used as temporary refuges in times of emergency. Exactly why three forts should be built in close proximity to each other is a mystery that may never be solved. Were they built at the same time? The siting of the two smaller forts on the hillsides suggests that the summit fort was already there, but if so why build two new sites instead of finishing off the existing one? Alternatively, it may be that the western fort is a 'hillslope enclosure' (like The Bulwark on Llanmadoc hill) and was deliberately built on sloping ground. The small ringwork may have been built next, followed by the hilltop enclosure which, for whatever reason, was never finished.

For the motorist there is only one way in and out of Llangennith village, but the visitor unfettered by cars can follow a number of public footpaths to the next destination, Llanmadoc. The most scenic route (at least on a clear day) is along the crest of Llanmadoc Hill, but a longer trail leaves the village in the direction of Broughton Bay, crosses the burrows at the north foot of the hill, and reaches Llanmadoc via Cwm Ivy. This track passes close to *Delvid farm* (57) a typical example of Gower vernacular architecture dating from the late 18th century, and displaying the by now familiar feature of a bed outshut. Delvid also has a recessed panel in the ceiling known as a 'charnel box', where meat was hung up to be cured. The box projects above the floor of the upper room and was used as the base for a bed.

At the camping ground just beyond Delvid a short detour can be made across the dunes to a bone cave at *Spritsail Tor* (58), which is marked on some OS maps as Prissen's Tor. The cave was discovered by quarrying in 1839 and lies in the seaward facing outcrop towards the north-east end of Broughton Bay. The front part of the cave has been destroyed, leaving two shallow chambers linked by a low passage. Artifacts recovered from excavations in 1839, 1849 and 1933 included a large number of animal remains, two pieces of worked bone of possible Palaeolithic date, and the skeletal remains of four humans of uncertain age. The only firm dateable finds were pieces of a Roman clay pot of the 3rd or 4th century AD.

Leaving Llangennith on the road to Burry Green, there is a signposted left turn after 2.5km which leads over Ryer's Down to Llanmadoc and

Kennexstone farmhouse, as reconstructed at St Fagans.

Cheriton. The group of agricultural buildings on the left of the junction is the site of *Kennexstone Farm* (59), one of the best known and most accessible vernacular buildings in Gower. But if you want to visit it then you must travel to the Museum of Welsh Life at St Fagans, where the building was reconstructed in 1953. Kennexstone was originally built around 1650 and consisted of just the hall, with an unheated attic bedroom above. Towards the end of the 17th century a kitchen was added, and the accompanying reconstruction drawing shows the house in this period. The difference between the two parts can be detected by the changes in the ceiling beams and roof trusses; the older part has a decorative scissor–tie truss, and the whole of the thatched roof has been lined on the underside with woven straw mats. In the kitchen there is a box-bedstead next to the fireplace and a charnel box in the ceiling. Late in the 18th century the house was refurbished and a second kitchen added; the interior has now been furnished in the style of the period c.1790 when Kennexstone was the home of the Rowlands family.

Llanmadoc (60)

The story of Llanmadoc begins in the Dark Ages when St Madoc, a student of the ecclesiastical college at Llangennith, established an oratory here in the 6th century AD. A number of other Gower churches claim a similar origin, but there is more concrete evidence than Medieval tradition to prove an Early Christian foundation here. The historian and rector of Llanmadoc, J. D. Davies, wrote that when the adjacent rectory was being repaired in 1861 part of an inscribed memorial stone was found embedded in the walls. This has now been reset in the windowsill of the nave, and has been stylistically dated to the late 5th-early 6th century AD. The Latin lines read 'Vecti Filivs Guani Hic Iacit', whcih translates as 'Vectus son of Guanus lies here'. Three years later another two stones were found in the graveyard wall and also removed for safe keeping to the church. One is a cube-shaped block carved with a simple cross on two sides, and the other is a larger slab roughly shaped into a plain pillar-cross. Both were set up in the period 600-800 AD as gravestones, though the smaller one may have been used as a boundary marker. Davies also mentioned that a battered Celtic handbell was ploughed up in a field nearby; further proof that Llanmadoc was a place of some importance to Early Christian society.

For most of the Medieval period the church belonged to the Knights Templar and Knights Hospitallers, two organizations of warrior monks set up to protect pilgrims on the hazardous journey to the Holy Land. Llanmadoc is one of the oldest and smallest churches still in use in Gower, and in all probability it was built soon after the manor was granted to the Templars in 1156. The round-headed chancel arch is a typical 12th century feature, but most of the surviving details belong to an overzealous restoration in 1865-6. The south porch and all the windows are modern, and so, too, is most of the chancel; but at the back you can see a joint in the stone-

Llanmadoc church.

work which marks where the old work finishes and the new begins. A 19th century etching of the unrestored interior shows that the present large east window replaced a single opening with a cusped head of 14th century type. The diminutive west tower is a late Medieval addition to the Norman nave, and has a restored saddleback roof with attractive stepped gables. Another feature shown on the etching and which still survives is a small door half-way up the wall beside the chancel arch. This was reached from the chancel by a step ladder and provided access to the rood-loft, which spanned the nave over the arch. According to Davies, parishioners who had transgressed against the church authorities were made to stand in this door during services as a public penance.

Echoes of the Medieval economy can be gleaned from the landscape around the village; there are characteristic strip fields east of the church, a place-name 'the conygaer' recalls a rabbit warren near Cwm Ivy, and on Whitford Burrows there are numerous heaps of cockle and oyster shells – proof that the flourishing Gower shellfish industry has a long history. Domestic rubbish of Medieval date has been found in some mounds, while others have produced finds dating as far back as the Bronze Age.

Llanmadoc Hill (61)

Several paths lead from the village green to the splendid vantage point of Llanmadoc Hill, 185m above sea level, where almost the entire length of the Gower peninsula can be seen on a clear day. The Bronze Age predilection for lofty burial places means that the hill is well peppered with round cairns – fourteen is a conservative estimate – and ranging from large heaps to insignificant stony patches. Great Cairn on the summit is the most notable of the group, measuring over 27m across and up to 1.8m high in places. Only blocks of red sandstone were used to build the mound, and it must have been a striking sight when completed. Another cairn worth

The Bulwark, Llanmadoc. An aerial view from the north-east with Llangennith and Worms Head in the background. (© Copyright reserved: National Monument Record for Wales).

tracking down lies on the north side of the hill about 250m below the crest of the ridge overlooking Broughton Bay. The covering mound has long been removed, exposing a central slab-lined burial cist 1.2m long.

The Bulwark. In the Iron Age a local tribe chose the hill as a suitable place to build a fortified settlement. For some unclear reason (perhaps out of deference to the Bronze Age graves) they built the fort away from the summit on ground sloping downhill to the east. A far from ideal defensive situation, but similar 'hillslope enclosures' are known from elsewhere (Hardings Down for instance) and so other factors may account for the choice of sites. The grass-covered rubble banks and rock-cut ditches form a complex pattern on the ground that can best be appreciated from an aerial photograph or a plan, and must surely represent work of more than one period.

There is an inner oval enclosure of about 0.9ha surrounded with a bank and ditch, and with an entrance gap on the east side. A sunken trackway flanked by additional ramparts leads up the hill to the gate. Almost surrounding this is a second line of defensive banks and ditches, which was never completed on the more steeply sloping north-east flank. Another rampart and ditch cut across the neck of the ridge on the more level western approach. The builders may have intended this outer bank to curve around the entire southern flank of the hill, and link up with the defence works at the east entrance. Despite the scale of the fort there are only a few surface indications of hut sites within the inner enclosure, but more might be revealed by future excavations. No large-scale archaeological work has been carried out at The Bulwark, though J. D. Davies dug up some animal bones, charcoal and stone tools in the 1870's.

Cheriton Church (62)

About 1km east of Llanmadoc the road to Llanrhidian dips down into the Burry valley and passes Cheriton, another Gower church which seems to have misplaced its village. There are only a few farms and cottages around, and nowhere is there anything you could call a centre. The existing building is dedicated to St Cadoc and was built around 1300, apparently as a replacement for an older church at Landimore destroyed, or abandoned, due to coastal flooding. The builders adopted the usual plan of a chancel, nave, and saddleback tower, but what makes Cheriton unique in Gower is the order in which they were put together. The tower stands between the nave and chancel, a very unusual arrangement for a small parish church and one that is generally found in buildings of a cruciform plan, such as a cathedral or monastery. If the builders intended to add balancing transepts on either side of the tower, then there is no sign that the work was ever started. The odd, but appealing, symmetry of the church has been spoiled somewhat by the addition of a vestry and south porch, though the latter does at least protect the finely carved 14th century nave door from weathering.

From inside, the effect of having a central tower is to lengthen the view,

Cheriton church.

further distancing the high altar from the gaze of the worshippers in the nave. The interior is dark and mysterious, dimly lit by rows of small lancet windows that have largely escaped modernization; even the modest east window (so often a target of overambitious restoration) has been left alone. On the outer side three weathered stone faces peer down at the visitor. The finely decorated choir stalls and altar rails were made by J. D. Davies, a skilled woodcarver in his own right, but best remembered today as the author of 'The History of West Gower'. He is buried just outside the porch. Davies undertook the restoration of Cheriton in 1874-5, and while stripping away the damp plaster he came across wall paintings of various periods including Tudor panels with biblical inscriptions, and Medieval imitation stonework with paired flower designs.

Cheriton was another church under the control of the Knights Hospitallers of St John, and they were probably responsible for building the adjacent *Glebe farm.* This privately-owned house was used as the parish rectory until the last century, and though it looks quite modern it is, in fact, the oldest domestic building in Gower. The only outward clue to its age is the octagonal chimney stack on the south wall, but internal features show that Glebe farm was a large and substantial Medieval house which was probably built around the same time as the church.

By stripping away the alterations and additions of later years it is possible to reconstruct the original appearance of the building, as it is shown in the accompanying drawing. The house was entered along a cross-passage with a service room at one side and the hall on the other. The smoke-blackened roof trusses are a clear indication that the lofty hall was originally warmed by a hearth on the middle of the floor. By the side of the high table a narrow stair passage led up to the *solar*, or private room, in a cross wing at the end of the hall. This comfortable chamber was the only one originally provided with a fireplace. There are other buildings adjoining the house and flanking a small courtyard on the west side, but they could be late Medieval additions. According to a survey of Glebe Farm compiled in 1720 there were five rooms in the house, 'all lofted save ye hall', with a barn, stable and brew house outside.

Across the valley from Glebe Farm stood *Cheriton Court*, the 16th century home of the Cradock family. The house was in ruins by the 1820's and J. D. Davies only saw an ivy-covered wall with an arched opening; accounts speak of wainscotted rooms with gilt ceilings, but now not a scrap remains.

North Hill Tor (63)
Just north of Cheriton the limestone escarpment ends in a dramatic outcrop called North Hill Tor, more familiarly known as Nottle Tor in Gower dialect. There is a footpath from the main road, and also a longer track along the base of the cliffs from Landimore village. Quarrying in the last century has reduced the north side of the rock to a sheer cliff, in the process destroying a small cave where Col. Wood discovered some flint tools of

Glebe Farm, Cheriton, as it may have appeared in the 14th century.

A suggested restoration of Landimore Castle.

Upper Palaeolithic date in 1869. During the Napoleonic wars the cave was supposed to have been used by local youths as a hideout when a press-gang boat was spotted on the river.

The landward side of the Tor is defended by a massive rubble bank and rock-cut ditch, which curves around the cliff from edge-to-edge. Traces of drystone walling would indicate that the bank was originally revetted with limestone blocks, making it an even more formidable barrier. The actual area enclosed is small compared to the scale of the defences, and this is more likely to be a Medieval ringwork than an Iron Age promontory fort.

Landimore Castle (64)

A short detour off the coast road brings you to the little village of Landimore, the 'church by the sea', a place-name which recalls a documented 13th-century church abandoned due to coastal flooding. High and dry on the hilltop above the village is Landimore or Bovehill castle, perhaps the most neglected and little-known Medieval ruin in Gower. No excavations have taken place here and the overgrown interior is not accessible to the public. This was once the centre of the largest manor on the peninsula, incorporating Llanmadog, Rhossili, Cheriton and coastal lands on either side of Weobley; though it was a Norman foundation the manor included a thriving Welsh community in the vicinity of Penclawdd and Wernffrwd. In the early 12th century the manor was held by the Turbervilles of Glamorgan, and ringworks at North Hill Tor and Cilifor (69) were built to control the territory. Isaac Hamon believed the castle had been built and inhabited by the De Breos family, but there is no evidence to suggest that the existing building is earlier than the 15th century, or that it occupies the site of an earlier earthwork castle. Hamon was nearer the mark in describing it simply as 'a large house', and in fact Landimore Castle is a fortified manor or 'stronghouse' rather than a fully-fledged fortress.

On December 4th 1451 the Duke of Norfolk and Lord of Gower, John Mowbray, gave the manor to Sir Hugh Johnys, and the grant is proudly recorded on Sir Hugh's memorial brass still to be seen in St Mary's church Swansea. Johnys was a veteran of the crusades, constable of Oystermouth, and the Duke's most trusted officer in Gower; in all probability he was responsible for building the castle. By the time Sir Hugh gained Landimore the great age of the feudal castle was almost over, and more effort was spent on domestic comfort rather than defence. Nevertheless, the unsettled political situation in the mid 15th century prompted at least some protective measures, and the ruined foundations of an outer enclosure with corner turrets can be traced in the field to the west.

The surviving upstanding walls define a long rectangular enclosure set on the edge of the hill, with various buildings ranged against the inner walls. A large building which crosses the enclosure and divides it into two courtyards was the great hall. The positions of the door and window openings reveal that it had a plan similar to Glebe Farm, with a lofty central hall and storeyed rooms at either end. There is a flanking turret on the south-east corner containing garderobes, and a 19th century cottage occupies the site of the gatehouse at the north end. According to J. D. Davies, Sir Hugh supplied the castle with water brought through lead pipes from a spring on Ryer's Down about a kilometre away. In the last century the remains of the pipe could be seen in the fields.

Weobley Castle (65)

Another Medieval castle lies barely 2km away from Landimore in an identical setting on a hilltop overlooking the Llanrhidian marshes, but this is no inaccessible, overgrown scanty ruin; Weobley is a substantial building open to the public and carefully preserved for posterity by CADW (Welsh Historic Monuments). One of the rooms also contains an exhibition on the archaeological sites and monuments of the Gower peninsula. Weobley is usually described as a fortified manor house and is perhaps the best example of such a building in Wales. The thin walls and wide, welcoming gateway would hardly 'laugh a siege to scorn', and in a document of 1410 it is referred to as a *manerium batellatum*, literally a battlemented manor. But the architectural evidence suggests that the builders started to construct a large and by no means insignificant stronghold, and that the original design was never carried through to completion.

The small lordship of Weobley was one of the earliest Norman territories established in Gower, though the actual site of the castle is believed to have been aquired at a later date by the De la Bere family (not to be confused with the De la Mares of Oxwich). John de la Bere (d. 1389) was the first

Weobley Castle: a view of the inner courtyard.

recorded holder of Weobley, though the family had been living in this part of Gower since the 13th century, and the thick-walled rectangular south-west tower surrounded by rock-cut ditches probably represents the remains of the first castle here. The earliest dateable masonry belongs to the late 13th century and consists of a two storeyed hall block, with high battlemented walls surrounding a central courtyard. There was a tower at the east corner (never finished) and signs that the walls were to continue further west and enclose a much larger area than at present. This work may have been carried out by David de la Bere, steward to De Breos, as a precautionary measure in the aftermath of the Welsh wars. The fact that the defensive perimeter was never completed suggests that either the builder ran out of money or, more likely, decided that there was no longer any pressing need for strong defences.

A few generations later, in the early 14th century, more buildings were added around the courtyard, including a solar, chapel and gatehouse. All the main buildings are two storeyed with the principal rooms on the upper floors over stores and basements. There is clearly a strong element of domestic comfort here, with all the residential apartments well provided with garderobes, fireplaces and spacious windows overlooking the Loughor estuary. However, glass being such an expensive commodity in the Middle Ages, only the upper part of the windows were glazed and the remainder was shuttered to keep out the draughts.

At the beginning of the 15th century the national uprising led by Owain Glyndŵr hit Gower, and the castle was in all probability captured and damaged by the rebels. A John de la Bere is believed to have been killed in the fighting. Once royal authority had been re-established the castle was repaired and the De la Beres were back in possession. But by the end of the century the manor had passed to Sir Rhys ap Thomas of Dinefwr, the most powerful Welsh magnate of the early Tudor period. Rhys carried out renovations and improvements on his various estates, and here at Weobley he built a porch and ante-room to create a more prestigious approach to the hall. But this proved to be an indian summer; by the middle of the 16th century Weobley was no longer the abode of wealthy and powerful lords, but merely a tenanted farmhouse, and by 1666 it had degenerated to the unenviable status of 'a decayed castle'.

Just across the road from the turning to Weobley Castle is a signposted public footpath to Manselfold. Follow this for about 400m and in the second field on the right after passing Windmill Farm will be seen one of the largest Bronze Age standing stones in Gower. This is *Sampson's Jack* (66), a 3.2m high block of millstone grit, now unfortunately very overgrown and robbed of its splendour by an encroaching hedgerow. The odd name might

Sampson's Jack standing stone.

be an allusion to the 6th century St Samson, who is reputed to have carved a cross on a Cornish standing stone to end its use as a pagan site. A number of megalithic monuments in Dyfed are similarly named after Samson. Two more standing stones lie a little way to the east in the vicinity of Oldwalls hamlet, though neither are accessible to the public. The first reached is a 2.2m high stone in a hedge just south-west of Pitton Cottage, while the other is a smaller stone also incorporated into a hedgerow, situated in a field north of the Greyhound Inn. Both can just be seen from the roadside.

Llanrhidian (67)

The church of St Illtyd and St Rhidian nestles on a rocky shelf above the marshes, a stern grey limestone building almost hidden from view by the old and new houses of the village, which seemingly tumble down the hillside in confusion. A narrow lane snakes its way down through the tangle of whitewashed buildings, and emerges onto the open expanse of the mudflats where it can be followed all the way to Crofty. Signs warn of flooding, but Llanrhidian church is high enough up the hill to avoid the watery fate of Landimore.

The building has a classic Medieval plan comprising a chancel, nave and west tower, with a south porch and north vestry added in the 19th century. In fact, much of the church we see today is a product of Victorian rebuilding, and apart from the rugged battlemented tower only the chancel displays some original unaltered work of the 14th century. A raised platform on one side of the tower parapet is known as the 'parson's bed', and is thought to have been used to light beacons warning of pirates on the estuary. The rebuilt walls of the nave contain a number of 18th century memorial slabs engraved with typically morbid lines commenting on the transience of life; 'Here lyeth my lifeless corps Bereved of living Breath' and the no less cheerfull 'Death with his Dart hath pierced my Heart' are just two examples.

Llanrhidian: one of the carved figures on the 9th century 'leper stone'.

Of far greater historical and artistic significance is the so-called 'Leper Stone' which was discovered around 1880 half buried in the ground beside the tower, and moved for safe keeping to the porch. It is a rectangular block of limestone about 2m long, one side carved with two stylised human figures flanked by a pair of even more surreal-looking animals. It almost certainly dates to the period 800-900 AD, but no one is quite sure what it represents, or whether it was a gravestone or the lintel of a doorway. An Irish influence has been detected in the style of the design, and a theory put forward by the Royal Commission on Ancient & Historical Monuments is that it represents St Anthony and St Paul meeting in the desert, a popular theme in Ireland. The Leper Stone is now the only tangible link with the Dark Age church, but in the late 17th century the great antiquarian and geologist, Edward Llwyd, sketched an inscribed stone which stood near one of the village mills. That stone is now lost but the Latin inscription, though badly copied or misinterpreted by Llwyd, would date it to the 5th or 6th century AD and the age of St Illtyd.

There were a number of grist and fulling mills in the vicinity of the church, all powered by the springs which gush out of the rock. Nether Mill is the oldest surviving, and bears a plaque dated 1803. Hamon mentioned that water from one of the springs was 'good for sore eyes', and he may have been referring to St Illtyd's well, which lies in a private garden of a house below the Dolphin Inn. The Annals of Margam Abbey record that in 1185 a 'copious stream of milk instead of water' flowed out of the well to the amazement of the villagers. Level-headed commentators have suggested that the miracle was nothing more than a froth of carbonate of lime! The entrance to the churchyard is guarded by two tall stone sentinels which have garnered some modern myths. The lower is a natural limestone slab which was set up in April 1844, according to the parish register, with the aid of a dozen men each fortified with a pint of beer. This is said to have been a Bronze Age standing stone, but though there are genuine monuments like Sampson's Jack in the vicinity, there is no record of how or where the stone was obtained. Similarly the upper stone on the green was erected in the early 19th century, and is claimed to have been a Dark Age cross later re-used as a pillory. There are metal staples in the top of the stone which seem to have been used for tethering something, but in all likelihood it is a pillar-cross of post-medieval date. it is hard to imagine any Dark Age sculptor labouring away on material as intractable as millstone grit!

Just past Llanrhidian village the B4271 branches off the main coast road and heads towards Killay and Swansea; after about 2km there is a sharp right turn which leads past Broad Pool and over Cefn Bryn to Reynoldston. In the triangle of land formed by this junction there is a solitary Bronze Age burial mound known as *Pen y Crug* (68), which may be an outlier of the main Prehistoric cemetary on Cefn Bryn. The mound is 24m across and 1.2m high and can best be seen early in the year before the summer bracken engulfs it. A central pit may have been dug by graverobbers or early antiquarians carrying out an unrecorded excavation.

From Pen y Crug the hump of *Cilifor Top* (69) can be seen on the skyline to the north, and although there is no public access to the hill good vantage points can be gained from both the B4295 and a minor road to Welsh Moor. The prominent earthworks visible on the slopes were built in the Iron Age to defend the hilltop settlement, which is the largest in Gower, occupying an area of almost 3 hectares. The steep natural slopes on the east side of the hill were overlooked only by a single rampart, but on the less precipitous flanks there were additional lines of closely spaced banks and ditches. Centuries of erosion and cultivation have reduced much of the defences to a series of level terraces or scarps, but excavations by William Morgan in 1910 revealed that beneath the innocuous-looking earthworks were rock-cut ditches up to 2.5m deep. No evidence was found to date the hillfort, although what Morgan described as red pottery could have been Roman samian ware, which was mass produced in Gaul and exported throughout the Empire.

Centuries after the Romans abandoned Britain, new invaders found a use for the old hillfort. A small bank and ditch ringwork was built by the Normans in the southern corner of the inner enclosure, utilising the earlier defences. Other examples of such 'hermit crab castles' can be seen at Caerwent, Cardiff and nearby Loughor (80). The Cilifor ringwork was probably built by the Turbervilles, who held extensive lands along the north coast of Gower in the early 12th century.

Once beyond Cilifor Top the limestone escarpment is left behind; the B4295 now passes through a landscape of sparse woodland and low hills rolling down to the marshlands bordering the wide estuary. Larger villages and more heavily populated areas are encountered on the way to Loughor, with correspondingly fewer ancient monuments surviving. Iron Age defended settlements crown the hilltops above Penclawdd and Blue Anchor, but they lie on agricultural land and are not really accessible to the public.

Also on private land, but situated next to the Llanrhidian caravan park is the intriguing site of the lost village and church of *Llanelen* (70). According to legend, the settlement was abandoned after the villagers helped save some sailors shipwrecked in the estuary, unaware that they carried a virulent plague. What survives today is the remains of a small nave and chancel building set on a levelled platform on the hillside. A rectangular building adjoining the churchyard wall may have been the dwelling of a priest. An archaeological group from Bristol have carried out some excavations here and discovered several graves, potsherds of 13th-14th century date, and traces of an older timber building beneath the surviving stonework. The church is believed to have fallen into disuse at some period in the early 13th century, and was later reoccupied as a farmstead. An outbreak of the Black Death in 1349 may have ended the existence of Llanelen, giving rise to the story mentioned above.

Part Two

NORTH GOWER

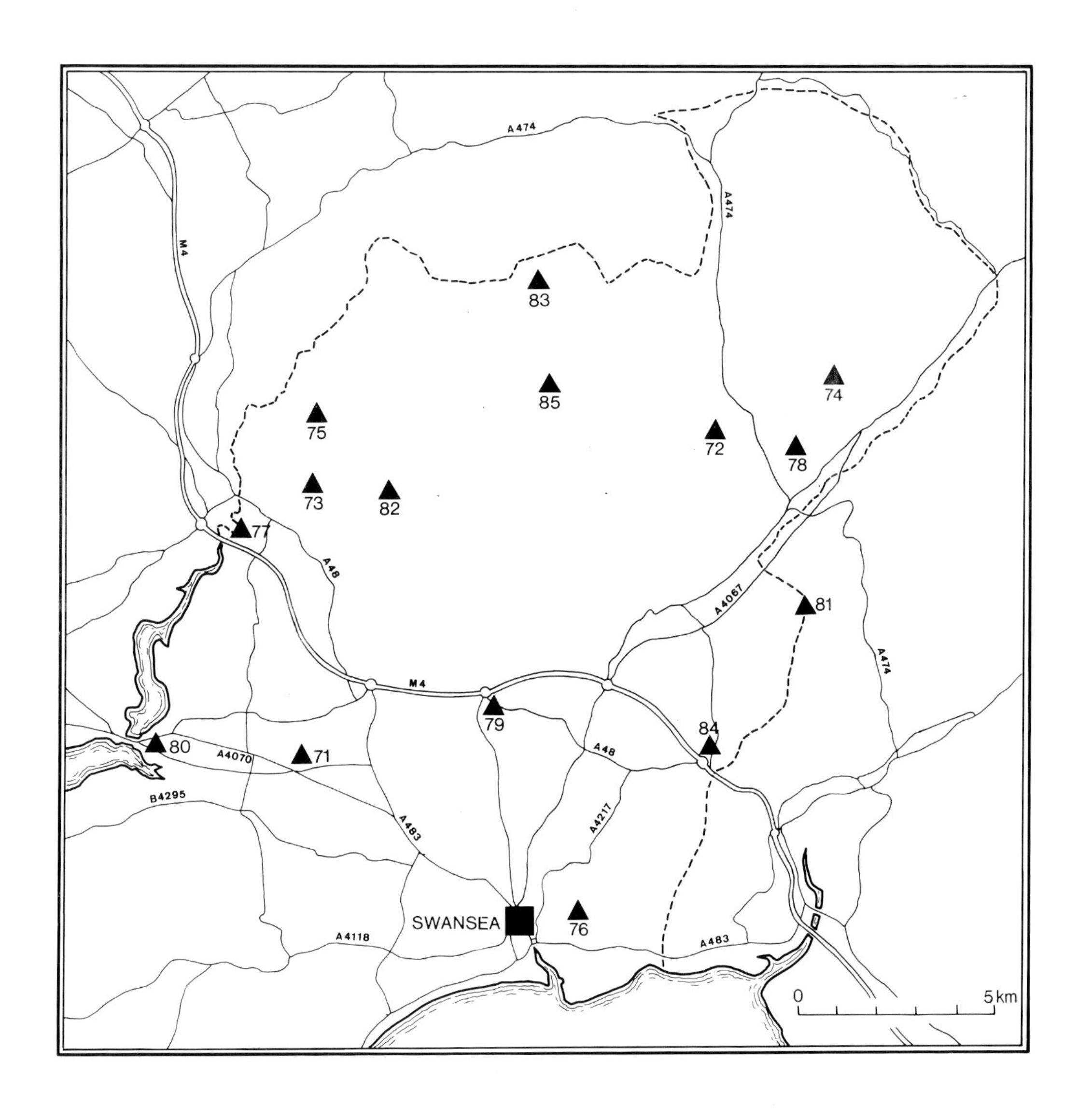

Although to most people 'Gower' signifies that unspoilt peninsula stretching west from Swansea, the centuries-old boundaries were very different and included the large upland parishes of Llandeilo Tal-y-bont, Llangiwg and Llangyfelach. The Medieval lordship of Gower bordered the Loughor river on the west, ran parallel to the Tawe on the east, and extended as far north as the mountaintops above Ystradgynlais and Glynamman. The small manor of Kilvey on the east bank of the Tawe was also annexed to Gower.

The topography and social history of this area is very different from that of the peninsula, and has closer affinity with the rest of the Glamorgan and Gwent uplands. During the Medieval period the land was nominally under the control of the Norman Lords of Gower, but the Welsh inhabitants were left very much alone, and their way of life changed comparatively little until the advent of the industrial age. The settlement pattern, too, is different here; there are few villages like Penrice or Llanrhidian, instead hill-farms and smallholdings dot the mountainsides, with the flatter valley floors taken over by housing and industrial development of the 19th and 20th centuries. But the hilltops and the moorlands are as empty as they have been for hundreds of years.

Because of the geography of 'North Gower' and the wider distribution of archaeological sites, it is not feasible to present a cohesive trail or a suggested itinerary. Instead this section of the book deals with the main sites and monuments accessible to the public and arranged in alphabetical order. Access to sites located on open moorland should present few obstacles, and the OS 'pathfinder' map No. 1107 will show the best roads and tracks to reach them.

Carn Goch (71)

East of Loughor the B4620 follows the straight line of its Roman predecessor as it climbs the grassy slopes of Carn Goch Common towards Swansea. In the angle between this road and the turning to the hospital are two small enclosures which are hidden by the undergrowth for much of the year. In winter it is possible to make out low square earthworks about 23-25m across with faint outer ditches, and one enclosure has an entrance gap in each side protected by an inturned bank, a feature known as a *clavicula*. These are Roman forts in miniature, built as a field exercise to keep the troops of *Leucarum* (80) in shape, hence the name 'practice camps'. There is another such camp on Stafford Common about 1.5km away, but it is possible that more could have been lost through ploughing and industrial development.

Less than a kilometre beyond the hospital is another overgrown earthwork that can just be seen from the roadside. This is Carn Goch, a much-damaged Bronze Age burial mound that now shares its heathland setting with a modern industrial estate. The process of destruction began as far back as c.1800, when the topmost layer of stones was robbed for road building, and what remained was dug up by J. T. D. Llewelyn in 1855. Beneath the covering mound of earth Llewelyn discovered a ring cairn with an off-

Carn Llechart.

centre burial cist. A further nine funerary urns with human remains were found outside the ring, along with votive pigmy cups and flint tools. With the limited evidence gained from the Victorian excavation it is difficult to say whether the internal structure of the cairn incorporated work of more than one period; nor is it certain if the burials represent a single mass grave or (as seems more likely) later burials inserted into the mound over a long period of time. Only re-excavation at some future date with more scientific methods may clarify the mystery of Carn Goch.

Carn Llechart (72)
In the past, monuments such as Carn Llechart were often considered to be 'Druidical circles', but this fine Bronze Age burial site is in fact much older than that notorious Celtic priesthood and, despite its present-day appearance, it is not a true stone circle. A ring of 25 thin slabs up to 0.9m high have been arranged in a rough circle about 14m across, and enclose a central burial cist. The area within the ring would originally have been filled in with loose stones. This belongs to a class of Bronze Age monument rather loosely identified as a 'cairn circle', which differ from ordinary round and ring cairns by having elaborate stone settings. Although many cairns have kerb stones around the edge to retain the stony covering mound, the size of the slabs used here point to a more ritual or ceremonial function.

Alongside an ancient trackway 400m north-west of Carn Llechart is a group of about 16 stony mounds of varying size, which appears to be the remains of a Bronze Age cemetery; were these the graves of less important tribespeople who wished to be buried in a privileged site close to the great cairn? The ridgeway was in use as a burial ground long before Carn Llechart was built, for there is a ruined Neolithic tomb a short distance to the south-

A reconstruction of two Platform Houses on Cefn Drum.

west. Only three slabs remain upright today and form a small burial chamber set up against a natural outcrop, with a displaced capstone on the east side. The poor preservation of the tomb may be due to the Bronze Age builders robbing materials for their cairns.

Carn Llechart can easily be reached from Pontardawe by taking the A474 to Ammanford, and then turning left at the pub in Rhydyfro village. After about 1.5km the road climbs the open mountainside and any number of paths can be followed up onto the ridgeway.

Cefn Drum (73)

When the undergrowth is low the extensive remains of a deserted Medieval settlement can be found on the slopes of Cefn Drum east of Pontardulais. The hill forms one arm of a horseshoe of high ground enclosing the upper end of the Camffrwd valley, and can be reached via several public footpaths off Upper Mill road and Dantwyn road. All over the south-facing slopes are ruined field walls, over forty cairns (probably just stone heaps resulting from agricultural clearance rather than Prehistoric burial mounds), and the foundations of about 17 long-houses. All the dwelling sites have been reduced to low stony earthworks, and may take quite a bit of tracking down. Ten belong to a distinctive type of Medieval upland dwelling known as a *platform house*, so called because the house was built on an artificially levelled terrace. The dwelling was a comparatively crude structure with turf or drystone walls and a turf or thatch roof, which has invariably decayed away over the centuries, leaving only the platform to mark its former existence.

Presumably, these platform houses and long-huts were occupied all year round, rather than shepherd's huts or *hafotai* occupied only during the summer months. But it is not certain how long the houses would have lasted in the British climate, nor whether the Cefn Drum group represents a fairly constant community, or just the homes of one or two Welsh families who would have moved into a new house every few generations.

Around nine house sites can be found between the electricity pylons and the start of a steep slope rising to the summit. There are two long–huts on the summit of the hill, and just beyond where the path dips down into a saddle between two peaks, there are three well marked platforms overlooking Cwm Dulais. Easiest of all to find (since the path crosses the platform of one) are two house sites on the west facing slopes of Twyn Tyle. From here the path descends to the moorland above Graig Fawr (75).

Cefn Gwrhyd (74)

Like many of the inter-valley ridgeways in upland Glamorgan, Cefn Gwrhyd was used as a natural trackway by ancient travellers, and the monuments and funerary relics left by those long-forgotten wayfarers lie scattered about the bleak mountaintop. A minor road snakes along the ridge, starting from the A474 at Rhydyfro and passing the turn to Llangiwg church (78). The road climbs onto the open moor, and after about 900m there is a gorse and heather covered mound on the left hand side. This is Carn Llwyd, now a rather unimpressive Bronze Age cairn, but according to antiquarian accounts it was once very similar to Carn Llechart (72), with three concentric rings of upright stones surrounding a central cist. By the time William Morgan saw it at the end of the last century only a few stones remained, and all have now disappeared.

There are about five more cairns along the ridge, but all lie some distance off the road and are not easy to locate without an OS map. A more obvious monument is a fallen standing stone which can be found on the right hand side, where the road begins to descend to Gwrhyd Chapel. The slab has been incorporated into a drystone wall on the edge of a field, and when first set up in the Bronze Age it would have stood at least 4m high, making it one of the tallest stones in Glamorgan.

Graig Fawr (75)

The broad moorland plateau of Graig Fawr extends north and west from Cefn Drum (73) near Pontardulais, and terminates in a high ridge overlooking the Loughor valley. During the Bronze Age, Graig Fawr was principally used as a vast cemetery, and the remains of more than forty cairns can be found scattered across the moor. Some of the mounds can be spotted easily enough, but many survive only as innocuous stony patches. On the eastern side of the moor, near the foot of Twyn Tyle, is a much larger monument consisting of a roughly circular enclosure 40m across, surrounded by two low banks of earth and stones, At one side of the enclosure is a small ring cairn about 10m across with a shallow outer ditch. The site could be interpreted as the remains of a dwelling hut and enclosure, though a ritual or ceremonial monument is perhaps a more likely explanation.

Despite the bleak location, Graig Fawr was home to a farming community in the Iron Age or Roman period, and the remains of their defended homestead can be seen on the highest part of the ridge overlooking the valley. All trace of a ditch has gone, but the inner rampart survives as a low bank enclosing an oval area 65-90m across. Centuries later in the Middle Ages another group of hardy farmers resettled the hill, and the remains of five platform houses lie on the slopes below the fort.

Kilvey Hill (76)

Over two centuries of heavy industry in the Swansea valley has defoliated Kilvey Hill, but in recent years tree planting by the Forestry Commission has returned some of the greenery to the slopes. The easiest way to reach the hill is via a footpath off Ty Draw road at Bon-y-maen, but it is worth making a short detour along Mansel road to see a 1.3m high Bronze Age standing stone, now in a very incongruous setting opposite a bus stop. As you climb the hill the earthworks of a small oval hillfort can be seen on the edge of a scarp ahead, and to the left, of the path. A more accessible fort lies a short distance further on, in a clearing on the right. Low earthworks define an oval enclosure 50-63m across, which was originally defended by a ditch between two banks. Excavations in 1968 brought to light a piece of 2nd century pottery from beneath the inner rampart, proving that the defences had been constructed well after the Roman conquest of South Wales.

The splendid viewpoint from the summit was probably one of the factors that influenced a local Bronze Age tribe to establish a cemetary here. There are four known cairns on the top, but only one can be easily reached today, and it lies some 200m east of the radio mast. The domed grassy mound is over 17m across and 1.5m high, though much of its height is accounted for by a windmill that was built on top of it in the late 17th century. Over the years the derelict stone tower has decayed away so that now only a short stump of curving wall remains. Another windmill tower survived until fairly recently at Cefn Hengoed near Bon-y-maen.

Llandeilo Tal-y-bont (77)

Since the construction of the M4 the motte and bailey castle at Llandeilo Tal-y-bont is in a very prominent position, and few travellers can fail to notice the bowl-shaped mound beside the motorway embankment on the south side of the river Loughor. This is the only motte in the lordship of Gower and it was built early in the 12th century by Henry de Villers to guard the first crossing upstream of Loughor castle. Another less obvious motte lies on the opposite bank in Dyfed. Given such a strategic location

Medieval cusped roof trusses at Llandeilo Talybont.

the castle must have been an obstacle for any invading army entering Gower from the west, but the only certain reference to it in the Welsh Chronicles is in an entry for the year 1215. A Welsh army led by Rhys Ieuanc burned Loughor castle and then 'made for the castle of Hugh de Meules at Tal-y-bont, and the garrison sought to hold it against him. But (Rhys) took it by force and burned some of the garrison and slew others'. De Meules rebuilt his castle and it remained in use well into the 14th century, as a reference to the *Turrym de Talebont* in 1319 makes clear. Whether there was actually a stone tower on the mound is doubtful, probably the defences were of timber throughout the entire life of the castle.

A small settlement grew up in the vicinity of the castle and the church of St Teilo, which is refered to in a document of 1396 as the *villa de Talband* and is now represented by a solitary ruined 18th-century farm. The 'church in the marsh' had suffered from flooding and damp for years, and when a more convenient church was built in Pontardulais in the mid 19th century, its fate was sealed. The deconsecrated building was left to rot away, a sad victim of decay and vandalism until, in 1984, a team of archaeologists unexpectedly discovered a series of rare wall paintings beneath the crumbling plaster. It was then decided to dismantle the church and remove it to the Museum of Welsh Life at St Fagans, there to be reconstructed and the conserved paintings reset on the walls. At the time of writing that has yet to be carried out, though some of the paintings have been on show to the public at the museum. They date from between the 15th and 18th centuries and depict biblical texts, figures of saints, and episodes from the life of Christ. Of all the paintings painstakingly removed from the walls the most remarkable is an illustration of Christ being spat upon by bystanders on the way to crucifixion, a scene which is quite startling in its coarse imagery.

Llandeilo has yet to be rebuilt at the museum and all that remains at present are some ruined walls within the raised circular churchyard on the marshy banks of the Loughor. The building displayed many phases of work from the 13th to the 18th centuries, with the earliest surviving masonry forming a simple rectangular chancel and nave. Around the beginning of the 15th century the church was extended on a fairly ambitious scale, with a large south aisle, porch and north chapel. More recent alterations involved the rebuilding of the chancel wall and the insertion of Gothic style windows.

The site of St Teilo's church can be reached along a public footpath marked 'Castell Du lane' which leaves the B4296 Gorseinon to Pontardulais road at the village of Waungron.

Llangiwg (78)

St Ciwg's church lies high on a mountaintop above the Tawe valley, remote from any town or village and with only a few lonely farms to keep it company. The devout congregation must have faced a long walk every Sunday. This is an unusual building and were it not for the leaning tower at the west end it might easily be mistaken for a typical 19th century Nonconformist chapel. There is no structural division between the nave and chancel, and all the windows are modern; even the tiny 'leper's window' in the east wall does not look very old. Above the door to the chancel is a plaque which reads 'This church was new roofed and considerably altered AD 1812' and this work probably accounts for the almost total lack of Medieval details. At the rear of the building, though, are two blocked windows with rounded heads which may be 16th century, and there is also a blocked arched doorway squeezed into the north-west corner beside the tipsy tower.

Around 1697 a local antiquarian, Thomas Morgan, wrote that the church

Llangiwg church.

was dedicated 'to an Hermit and saint by tradition named Kiwg, who had his cell in a rock anext to the churchyard over which rock there is at ys day a little house built for the parish clerk'. There is no sign of this 'cell' today, but perhaps Morgan was imaginatively referring to the overhanging crags just north of the church.

There is some evidence to back up the claim that Llangiwg was a Dark Age foundation, for among the graves opposite the porch is a large block which once held a memorial stone of the period 800-1100 AD. A more obvious Early Christian monument in the form of a round slab incised with a simple cross, can be seen in the porch, but in fact this was brought here from Gellionnen Chapel on the far side of the Clydach valley sometime in the 18th or early 19th century. The slab is only the top part of a 9th-century pillar cross which the antiquarian Edward Llwyd saw intact c.1693. It was standing on a Bronze Age cairn near the chapel but could have been moved from a nearby lost church of Llan Eithrim, which survived only as foundations when visited by William Morgan in the 1890's. The cross must have been damaged prior to 1800, when the lower part was incorporated into the rebuilt walls of the chapel. The carvings depict a man with upraised arms, wearing a stylised garment or cape decorated with knotwork designs. This has now been removed for safe keeping to the Swansea Museum.

Llangiwg can be reached off the A474 road from Pontardawe to Ammanford, by taking a right turn at Rhydyfro village. After 1km there is a right hand turn to the church; the road ahead crosses the ridge of Cefn Gwrhyd.

Llangyfelach (79)
For over 160 years the bell tower and the parish church of Llangyfelach have stood apart from each other, a curious situation that has prompted a

Llangyfelach church tower: the base of a 10th century cross can just be seen to the right.

rustic joke about the tower being 'the first dissenter in Wales'! According to a folk-tale the Devil tried to hinder building work by stealing the materials, but when he tried to fly off with the newly-completed tower a priest made the sign of the cross and frightened the Devil into dropping it where it now stands. But the reasons for the separation are much more mundane than that. Towards the end of the 18th century the Medieval church was in a bad state of repair, and its end was hastened by a violent storm in the 1800's. By 1829 only the tower and chancel remained, and in the following year a new church had been constructed out of the old tithe barn which stood nearby.

On the east face of the tower there is a blocked archway which probably led into the vanished nave; however, there is some evidence to suggest that the tower was always detached from the main body of the church like certain Herefordshire churches and (if the Dineley drawing is correct) St Mary's in Swansea. But the origins of St Cyfelach's church go much further back in history than the Middle Ages and there are three carved stones which confirm the documentary evidence of a 6th-century Christian foundation. Above the north door of the tower there is a re-set gravestone with an incised ring-cross of 9th century date. During restoration work in 1913 another gravestone was found under the floor of the nave and set on the north wall (a modern replica adorns the lych gate). This has a simple but elegant plaitwork ring-cross with the Latin inscription CRUX-XPI 'the cross of Christ'.

The finest monument here is the pedestal of an early 10th century pillar cross which stands next to the tower, and is decorated with intricate knotwork panels. The cross head is unfortunately lost, but it would have been as richly decorated as the base and stood as much as two or three metres high. Complete examples of this type of sculptured stones can be seen at St Illtyd's church Llantwit Major, and the Margam Abbey museum. According to the 'Life' of St David written down in the 12th century, the *Monasterium Langemelach* was one of twelve sites established by the patron saint of Wales, and the unusually large and rounded churchyard may reflect the boundary of that monastic settlement.

The Welsh name for such an establishment is a *clas*, and until comparatively recent times this name lingered on to refer to the whole manor. The 16th century antiquarian Rice Merrick wrote 'within Clas sometime stood an old pile or castle, Y Llan, now all in ruin. Within it stand the two ancient houses of the Hopkins, viz Ynysdawy and Ynysforgan'. Whatever 'Y Llan' was has not survived, but the other two houses remained until more recent times. Ynysforgan was rebuilt in the 17th century and has been recorded in detail by the Royal Commission on Ancient and Historical Monuments. Isaac Hamon described Ynystawe as 'a very ancient house (but much decayed) ... [with] a spacious hall beside many other Roomes'. Evidently it was a Medieval building of some size, but it was rebuilt as a Gothic mansion in the 19th century and finally demolished in 1960. Llangyfelach church is situated beside M4 junction 46, and can also be reached from the city centre via the B4489 and A48.

A fragment of decorated Samian pottery from Roman Loughor.

Loughor (80)
The village of Loughor lies on a ridge overlookin the lowest crossing point of the river and the western approach to Swansea and the Gower peninsula. The strategic value of such a location was recongnised more than 19 centuries ago when the Romans built a fort here, as part of a chain of military bases encircling the potentially troublesome tribes living in the uplands of South Wales. Antiquarians and historians have long known of the existence of *Leucarum* since it is listed in the Antonine Inventory (a sort of Roman AA guide to forts) as being located between *Moridunum* (Carmarthen) and *Nidum* (Neath). Roman artifacts have been discovered nearby, and construction work on the railway in 1852 uncovered the foundations of a bath house. But it was only during excavations on the Medieval castle in 1968-69 that the actual perimeter of the fort was recorded. Further work was carried out in 1970-73, and also between 1982-88 to recover as much information as possible before the western side of the fort was destroyed with the building of the A484 Llanelli link road. Nothing can be seen of the fort above ground today, but the excavations carried out by the Glamorgan-Gwent Archaeological Trust in the 1980's were open to the public.

Leucarum was built c.AD 74-76 to a tried and tested plan consisting of a round-cornered oblong enclosure of about 2.3 hectares surrounded with an earth bank and outer ditch. In the first quarter of the second century AD the rampart was reinforced with a masonry wall with several watch towers along the perimeter; the footing of one such tower was found beneath the castle. Within the fort there would have been two main roads, the *via principalis* and *via praetoria,* which crossed at right angles and led to gateways in each side of the enclosure. Besides the intersection stood the most important building, the *principia* or headquarters, and the remainder of the space would have been taken up with barracks, stores, granaries, workshops, and the like. In the western part of the site the Trust found the stone foundations of a large building with several suites of rooms arranged around a central courtyard, with a verandah along the roadside. This was interpreted as the commander's house or *praetorium.*

The fort was subsequently reduced in size and the unwanted western third cut off with a bank and ditch. This may have occured around AD 130, but before long Leucarum was abandoned for well over a century before it was reoccupied between 275-310 AD. The only evidence we have for any further activity at Leucarum between the departure of the Romans and the arrival of the Normans is a single carved block of stone now kept at the Swansea Museum. The stone is a reused Roman altar with several notches and grooves along one side, which is actually an Irish script known as *ogham.* Many ogham messages were scrawled on gravestones in western parts of Wales and record the presence of Irish settlers in the 5th and 6th centuries AD. Perhaps the derelict, overgrown fort sheltered an immigrant family for a time, or there may have been an Early Christian burial ground here.

Soon after Henry de Beaumont established Swansea castle, his steward, Henry de Villers, was given leave to build castles on the western approach to the lordship. De Villers built a motte and bailey at Talybont (77) and a ringwork at Loughor which was sited above the south-east corner of the fort Rampart. The excavations of 1969-73 revealed a succession of stone and timber buildings within the enclosure as well as the possible foundations of a keep. At the end of the 12th century a stone wall was built on top of the ringwork bank, but this failed to hold back a Welsh attack in 1215. The defences were further modified at the very end of the 13th century, when the old keep was replaced with a small residential tower which had two basic but habitable chambers above a ground floor storeroom. The tower also served to guard the entrance gate which lay immediately adjoining the south side. This was probably the work of William de Breos III who was also engaged in rebuilding Swansea castle after a Welsh attack in 1287, but it could also have been built by his steward, John Iweyn, who was granted Loughor in 1302. A century later, the Glyndŵr uprising reached Gower, and the modest defences of the castle would have been no match for the rebel army. By the 16th century Loughor was apparently derelict and in decay, and today only three walls of the tower remain upstanding, and all the other stonework lies buried beneath the turf on top of the mound.

Mynydd Drumau (81)

Pick a clear day to explore the 270m high ridge of Mynydd Drumau, for the views of Gower and the Glamorgan coast are quite impressive. A public

Carreg Bica standing stone.

footpath starts from the 'Coach House' on the Drumau road between Birchgrove and Neath Abbey, and climbs up through the woods to emerge on the bare hilltop. There are several Bronze Age cairns on the ridge, but the most prominent relic is *Carreg Bica*, a 4.3m high monolith which is the tallest standing stone in Glamorgan. A few metres to the north is the remains of a small cairn; were the two monuments connected?

At the far end of the field beyond the cairn the path veers to the south and begins to slope downhill, passing a group of four Medieval platform houses. If you continue along the crest of the ridge, keeping to the drystone wall, another group of huts will be found in the second field beyond. The more prominent earthworks in this field are the remains of five *pillow mounds*, comprising low earthwork banks with side ditches, which were constructed for rabbits to burrow in. The tithe map of 1841 names the surrounding field as the 'old warren' indicating that there was a rabbit farm here at one time.

Cross to the lower (west) end of the field and there is a footpath between two fences which leads back to Carreg Bica, and passes the remains of a large round cairn after about 400m. A modern wall crosses one side of the mound, but it is otherwise in a good state of preservation, with the central stone lined cist exposed to view. From here the path heads southwards across open moorland to the standing stone.

Penlle'r Bebyll (82)

Penlle'r Bebyll, the 'high place of the encampment' is one of several puzzling earthworks in the mountains between Pontardulais and Pontardawe. The site consists of a low bank with a slight outer ditch enclosing a level area about 17m across. There is a wide entrance gap on the south side, which is partly blocked by a smaller oval enclosure. The name led William Morgan to suggest it was a Medieval encampment built to contain plague victims, and the surface features do look like a small dwelling hut with an adjoining yard or cattle pound. However, the setting is very remote and inhospitable, and a Prehistoric date is perhaps more likely. Penlle'r Bebyll may have been an elaborate ritual enclosure of the type also found on Cefn Bryn (34), Graig Fawr (75), and Tor Clawdd (85). It lies near the summit of Mynydd Pysgodlyn on the left hand side of a minor road from Felindre to Cwm Dulais.

Penlle'r Castell (83)

This is one of the most remote archaeological sites in Gower, located on a mountaintop in the midst of uninhabited moorland on the northern boundary of the lordship; and this location gives a clue to the age and function of the site. Despite early theories of an Iron Age or Roman origin Penlle'r castell is certainly a Medieval castle, albeit an untypical one, and the most likely reason put forward to explain its presence in this distant spot is that it was built in the second half of the 13th century by William de Breos II during a territorial dispute with his Welsh neighbour, Rhys Fychan of Dinefwr. From this location De Breos could stamp his authority on the surrounding wastelands and oversee any military action taking place on the northern fringes of his territory. Rhys' stronghold at Carreg Cennen could also be glimpsed through a gap in the Black Mountain.

Despite such a late date the castle defences are rather old-fashioned, but this may be a case of the builders having to make do with whatever materials were to hand. There is a low oval mound rather like an oversized motte 34m long by 18m across, surrounded by a deep ditch. Another ditch cuts into the mound effectively separating it into two unequal parts, and William Morgan thought this was a later quarry dug by roadworkers in search of building stone. However, it seems more likely that it was an original defensive feature separating the keep from the other buildings in the bailey. All structures on top of the mound have been reduced to stony earthworks, though the outlines of three rectangular buildings can be discerned. There is no documentary history about the castle, and even early antiquarians could offer little help; Rice Merrick writing c.1584 dismissed it with the sparse comment 'Ller castle now in utter ruine'. Perhaps some future excavation will uncover the secrets of this enigmatic site.

Penlle'r Castle lies just off the mountain road from Clydach to the Amman Valley, at the northern end of Mynydd y Gwair. Just where the road passes its highest point and begins to dip down towards Ammanford you will need to walk across the moor in a north-easterly direction for about 200m to get to the site.

Scott's Pit, Llansamlet (84)

The gaunt shell of Scott's pit engine house stands close to the east bound carriageway of the M4 near Llansamlet, and can be reached along Gwernllwynchwyth Road just off junction 44. Although the subject of industrial archaeology is really beyond the scope of this book, the building deserves to be included as a memorial to the dwindling remains of the old Swansea valley industries. Coal was mined at Kilvey Hill as far back as the 14th century, and by the 17th century Swansea was considered to be the third largest coal producing area in Britain. The early mines were shallow pits or tunnels dug as far as the water level allowed, and deep mining only became possible with the advent of efficient mechanical pumps to drain the workings.

Scott's pit was sunk in 1817-19 by John Scott, a London solicitor, who later sold the property to a local coalowner, C. H. Smith. Smith's venture lasted until 1842, but the tall building used to house the steam driven pump was re-used in 1872 to drain a nearby mine, until its final closure in 1930. These engine houses are a familiar feature of the Cornish landscape, but a large number are also known in Wales , many now crumbling and forgotten in long-disused mining areas. The tall chimney stack served a boiler pro-

Scott's Pit engine house.

viding steam for the engine, which was contained in the adjoining tower block. The engine transmitted the slow power of a piston to a pump rod in the mine shaft, by way of a huge rocking beam which rested on the outer wall of the building. By the action of this vast 'see-saw', water was drawn up the shaft through a series of hollow plungers. It is estimated that a beam engine at Landore could pump up 100 gallons per stroke, at a rate of 12 strokes a minute.

The derelict building was conserved in 1976-80 and can now be safely explored by visitors; but only a short distance away is another engine house of greater historical importance which has yet to be preserved for posterity. The short-lived mine at Gwernllwynchwyth was sunk between 1772-82 and abandoned only a few years later in 1786. The crumbling and overgrown building stands next to the road near Peniel Green, and its importance lies in the fact that it housed a rotative, or winding, engine (rather than a pump) some time before the inventor James Watt is credited with developing successful rotary motion.

Tor Clawdd (85)

Tor Clawdd is the name of an isolated hilltop at the upper end of the Lliw Valley, overlookin Cwm Clydach and the lonely moors stretching north to Ammanford. The 'clawdd' element of the place name refers to an earthwork dyke which runs for about 1000m around the north facing edge of the hill. This was probably built in the 8th or 9th century AD, at a time when many other boundary banks were being constructed in upland Glamorgan, perhaps to define newly organized territories or serve as short-lived military obstacles. A raised causeway crosses the hill towards the dyke and this is part of an ancient trackway from Swansea to Llandeilo. Close to this road is an earthwork ring 16m across and surrounded by a low bank with a shallow outer ditch. There is an entrance gap on the south-east side. The proximity of this ring to the dyke may indicate it was connected in some way, possibly a camp site, though perhaps it was a large ring cairn or ritual enclosure of Bronze Age date. Tor Clawdd can be reached off the mountain road to Ammanford from either Clydach or Morriston hospital, and which also passes close to Penlle'r Castell.

Part Three

SWANSEA

The city of Swansea lies on the west bank of the river Tawe guarding the approach to the Gower peninsula, an evergrowing urban giant seemingly at odds with its largely unspoilt neighbour. A visitor to Swansea could be forgiven for thinking it a modern city, so thorough has been the rebuilding over the last 150 years. Biggest culprit of all was the *luftwaffe*, which flattened much of the centre in February 1941, but blame must also be heaped on the Victorian town planners for allowing the demolition and rebuilding of entire streets and run-down areas. Today there are only two buildings of Medieval origin still surviving, the Cross Keys Inn and part of the castle, and only old photographs and illustrations remind us of what has been lost.

History

The story of Swansea really begins around 1106 when Henry de Beaumont, Earl of Warwick, arrived here and built a castle to defend the territory and act as the administrative centre of the Norman lordship. What was here before the 12th century is less certain. According to tradition a Viking named Sweyne founded an outpost in the ninth century, giving rise to the place-name 'Sweyne's ey' (meaning island or islet), and there may also have been an Early Christian church here dedicated to St Cenydd. But the impetus for the growth of Swansea as a town was clearly down to the Normans. Earl Henry's castle was up and

The New Castle, Swansea.

Cutaway reconstruction of the New Castle, Swansea.

running by 1116 when a Welsh army attacked, but the garrison put up a stout resistance and only the 'outer castle' was burned. This either refers to the early town enclosure or, more likely, the bailey of the earth and timber castle. Another attack took place in 1192 when Swansea endured a ten-week siege, but the Welsh were more successful in 1215 and 1217 and the castle was destroyed. The defences still relied on deep ditches and earthworks topped with palisades, but at some time in the early 13th century a stone wall with at least one square flanking tower was built, and this in time became known as the Old Castle. Nothing of this work survives above ground today, but the masonry foundations and remains of the mound were noted during clearance in 1913.

There were two further recorded attacks in 1257 and 1287 when the town, and perhaps the castle as well, was burnt. Within a few years the Lord of Gower, William de Breos II began to construct the '*New Castle*' in the south-east corner of the bailey, and this now forms the surviving part of Swansea castle. The buildings were apparently separate and independent of the Old Castle, and consisted of a main residential block with a hall and domestic chambers at first floor level above vaulted basements. There was a courtyard on the north side enclosed by high walls, with a two-storied square tower on the east corner. The most striking feature of the castle is the row of elegant dressed stone arches on the outer side of the hall block, which carries the battlemented wall-walk above the rooftops. This distinctive architectural feature is only known elsewhere at the Bishop's palaces at St David's and Lamphey in Dyfed, both built by Henry de Gower in the early 14th century.

Bishop Henry (c.1278-1347) was, as his name implies, a native of these parts, and was responsible not only for undertaking building work at St David's Cathedral but also here at Swansea and Llanddewi. There is a long-standing tradition that the New Castle was another episcopal residence, but there is no convincing evidence to prove this; some historians think it likely that the arcaded parapet was an embellishment added in the 1330's by Henry's masons (then at work on the nearby Cross Keys Inn) for the Lord of Gower, John de Mowbray. There is still a mystery as to why Mowbray, an absentee landlord, should want to spend money on such a purely decorative feature. In the early years of the 15th century Swansea castle endured another bout of military action when it was captured by the army of Owain Glyndŵr, but by the late 16th century it was in decay, and a survey carried out in the following century described it as an 'ancient decayed building called the New Castle'. The Old Castle was apparently in an even worse state for the survey refers to it as 'a piece of ruinous building'. During these declining years the castle was variously used as a town hall, a glass factory, debtor's jail, post office, and a newspaper office. new buildings went up and old ones were adapted, and it is surprising that anything ancient has managed to survive at all!

The Town

The Medieval town surrounded the castle on all sides except the east, where the land sloped down to the river and quay. modern harbour developments have affected the course of the Tawe, and the river no longer flows beneath the castle walls. Murage grants were issued by the Crown in 1317 and 1338 which enabled tolls to be collected to meet the cost of replacing the timber defences of the borough with stone walls. The line of the town walls has been deduced from early maps and from buried foundations noted in modern excavations, and comprised a stone wall fronted with a ditch, with three or four gateways. The accompanying map shows the approximate location of the walls superimposed onto the modern day street layout.

In St Mary's Street will be found the only remaining domestic building in Swansea, the *Cross Keys Inn*, which has recently been extended in a mock-Medieval style. The twin gabled façade is a 1950 restoration of

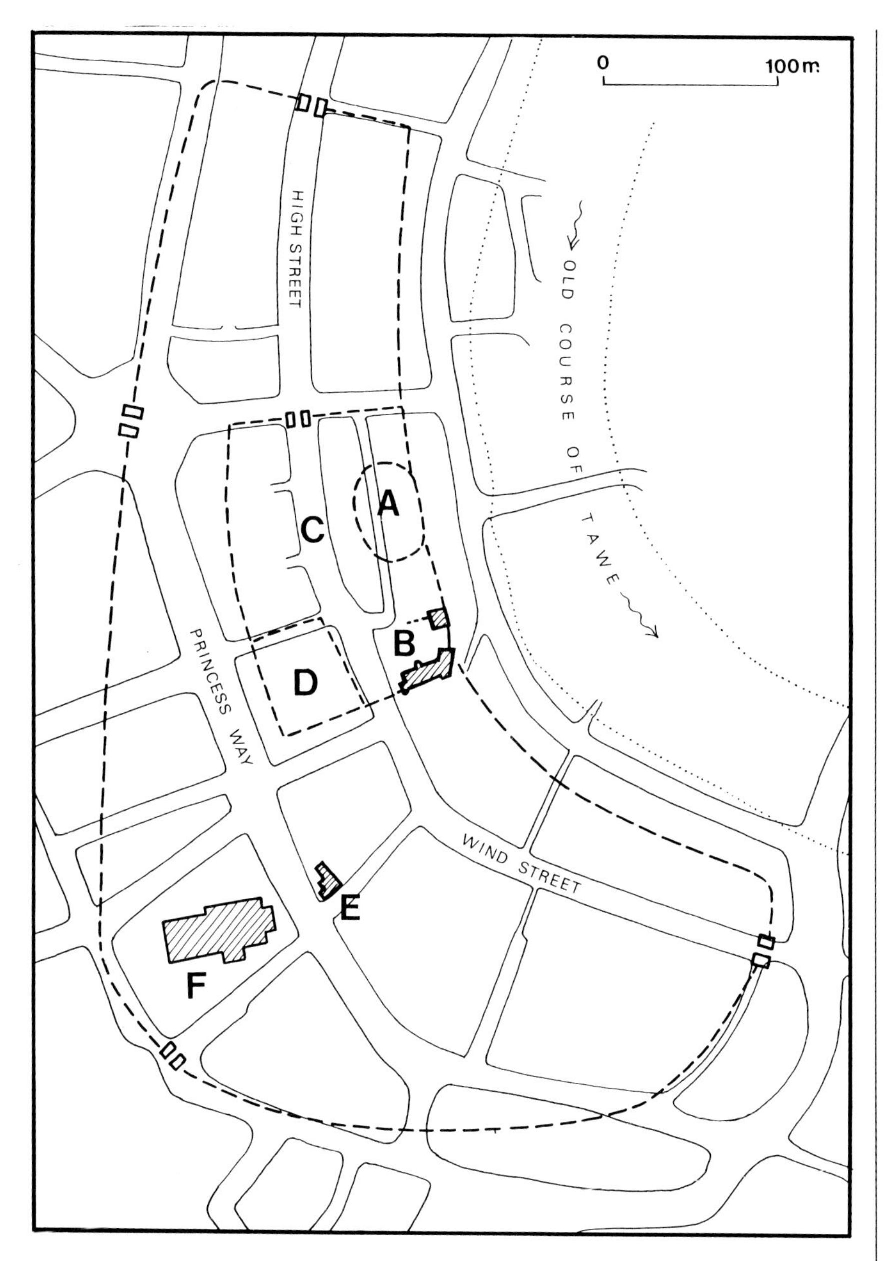

A: The Old Castle
B: The New Castle
C: Castle bailey
D: The Plas
E: The Cross Keys Inn
F: St Mary's Church

the early 17th century frontage, when the building was divided into two ground floor shops; but around the back of the inn are three 14th century windows which reveal the real age of the Cross Keys. In 1332 Bishop Henry de Gower founded a 'hospital' or almshouse 'For the support of other poor chaplains and laymen deprived of bodily health', and the Cross Keys Inn is the only surviving part of that worthy establishment. The original function of this building is not known for certain, but the fireplace on the first floor and an open roof with carved beams

Cross Keys Inn: the restored 17th century frontage seen from St Mary's Street.

suggests that it was a domestic hall, perhaps the residence of the chaplain or attendant priests. At the Reformation the hospital was suppressed and the property purchased by Sir George Herbert who is thought to have removed materials from the site for use in building his 'New Place'.

Lost Buildings

As late as the beginning of the 19th century the centre of Swansea had not grown beyond the limits defined by the Medieval walls, and many early buildings still survived. A few lingered on to be photographed in the second half of the century, such as the Old Post Office (Goat St), the Beaufort Arms (West Bank) and the Old Carmarthen Arms (College St) which appears to have been of late Medieval date and stood on the site of the north castle gate.

St Mary's Church still stands in the heart of the city, but the existing structure dates from 1954-59 and is a reconstruction of the Victorian church which was damaged in the last war. The earliest representation of the church is a drawing of 1684 by Thomas Dineley who depicted a large nave with a detatched tower and chancel. If the drawing is taken at face value then either the building was partly ruined at the time, or the tower was freestanding, like certain churches in Herefordshire. In 1739 the first major rebuilding took place and the old nave was replaced by a huge and ugly classical edifice which survived until the last decade of the 19th century. William Morgan surveyed the old church during demolition and his notes and photographs were published in his 'Antiquarian survey of East Gower' (1897). Only the tower and chancel survived of the Medieval building, with the 16th century Herbert chapel on the north side. In the chancel there were tomb recesses and arched wall seats where the priests sat during intervals in the long services. St Mary's contained two important monuments to past worthies, the most impressive was a tomb with sculptured effigies of Sir Matthew Cradock

A conjectural reconstruction of The Plas, based on details recorded prior to the destruction of the site.

(1468-1531) and his wife, Lady Catherine Gordon, shattered in the blitz and subsequently broken up. Fortunately a memorial brass to Sir Hugh Johnys (died c.1485) has managed to survive, though the tomb it formerly adorned has not; in 1846 it was removed and the grave opened to reveal the 'mouldering remains' of Sir Hugh and his wife. *Sic transit gloria mundi.*

By far the most important building lost to redevelopment was New Place, also known as *The Plas*, which stood in the south-west corner of the bailey on a site now occupied by castle gardens. This large rambling mansion was a derelict shell by the time of its demolition in 1840, but several illustrations and two models (one still surviving in Swansea Museum) fortunately record its appearance. The Plas originated in the 14th century when parts of the castle bailey were sold off for commercial development but most, if not all, of the building was put up by Sir Matthew Cradock at the beginning of the 16th century. There were various buildings arranged around three sides of a small courtyard, with a gatehouse on the east facing the New Castle. On the north stood the great hall, a magnificent building with a high roof of carved timbers, and an adjoining three storied tower block. The scale of The Plas and the lavish use of carved stones for the doors and windows would have contrasted with the humbler town buildings around, and signalled to all the wealth and social standing of the Cradocks.

Swansea Museum (Open daily except Mondays & Sundays)
The museum of the Royal Institute of South Wales is an imposing neoclassical building just off Victoria Road, which was opened to the public in 1845, the first museum in Wales. The archaeological gallery now contains a selection of finds and artifacts from the Swansea area illustrating all the major historical periods. Exhibits include flint tools and animal bones from Paviland (40) and Minchin Hole caves (10); Bronze Age funerary urns from Carn Goch (71); Roman pottery from Loughor (80); a ninth century sculptured stone from Gellionnen (78), and a bronze incense burner discovered in the ruins of Penmaen church (19). There are also displays on natural history, geology, the Swansea pottery industry, and a newly opened gallery devoted to the museum's most famous resident, an Egyptian mummy.

REFERENCES AND FURTHER READING

The following selection of published works provided much of the factual information contained in the text, and are standard reference sources for anyone interested in delving deeper into the history of Gower. Long out of print, but containing valuable archive material are the archaeological surveys by J. D. Davies and William Morgan; more up to date work has been carried out by the Royal Commission on Ancient and Historical Monuments (RCAHM). In addition many articles on Gower sites can be gleaned from the pages of yearly journals such as *Archaeologia Cambrensis* (Journal of the Cambrian Archaeological Association), *Morgannwg* (The Journal of Glamorgan History) and of course, *Gower* (The Journal of the Gower Society). The list of books has been split up into categories for the reader interested in a particular historic period.

PREHISTORIC

Caves of Gower. B. Morris (Gower Society 1971)
Glamorgan Inventory, vol. 1, part 1. RCAHM (HMSO 1976)
Gower Caves. E. E. Allen & J. G. Rutter. (Swansea 1948)
Prehistoric Gower. J. G. Rutter (Swansea 1948)
Glamorgan County History, vol. II, ed. H. N. Savory (Cardiff 1984)

ROMAN AND DARK AGE

Glamorgan County History, vol. II
Glamorgan Inventories, vol. 1, parts 2 & 3. RCAHM (HMSO 1976)
The Roman Frontier in Wales. V. E. Nash-Williams (University of Wales Press 1954)
Wales in the Early Middle Ages. Wendy Davies (Leicester University Press 1982)

MIDDLE AGES

Castles of Gower. B. Morris (Gower Society 1970)
Glamorgan County History, vol. III, ed. T. B. Pugh (Cardiff 1971)
Glamorgan Inventory, vol. 3, parts 1 & 2. RCAHM (HMSO 1991 & 1982)
Gower Churches. G. Orrin (Rural Deanery of West Gower 1979)
Noteworthy Gower Churches. L. A. Toft (Gower Society 1981)

POST-MEDIEVAL

Glamorgan County History, vol. IV, ed. G. Williams (Cardiff 1974)

Glamorgan Inventory, vol. 4, parts 1 & 2. RCAHM (HMSO 1981 & 1988)
Guide to the industrial archaeology of the Swansea region. S. Hughes & P. Reynolds (Association for Industrial Archaeology 1988)
Houses of the Welsh Countryside. P. Smith (HMSO 1988)
Industry before the Industrial Revolution. W. Rees (Cardiff 1968)

SWANSEA

A Pictorial History of Swansea. W. C. Rogers (Gwasg Gomer 1981)
Swansea, an illustrated history, ed. G. Williams (Christopher Davies 1990)
Swansea castle and the Medieval town. Edith Evans (Swansea City Council and Glamorgan-Gwent Archaeological Trust 1983)
The City of Swansea, challenges and changes, ed. R. A. Griffiths (Alan Sutton 1990)

GENERAL

A Gower Anthology, ed. D. Rees (Christopher Davies 1977)
An Antiquarian Survey of East Gower. W. Ll. Morgan (London 1899)
Glamorgan Historian, vols. 1-12, ed. S. Williams (D. Brown & Sons)
The Buildings of Wales: Glamorgan. J. Newman (Penguin/University of Wales Press 1995)
The History of West Gower, vols. 1-4. J. D. Davies (Swansea 1877, '79' 85 '94)
A Portrait of Gower. Wynford Vaughan-Thomas (Hale 1976)

ANTIQUARIAN SOURCES

British History: Nennius, trans J. Morris (Phillimore 1980)
Brut y Tywysogion. (Anon) trans T. Jones (Univeristy of Wales Press 1952)
Description of Gower, July 1697. Isaac Hamon (reprinted in *Transactions of the Cymmrodorion* 1965)
Itinerary of John Leland 1536-1539, ed. L. T. Smith (London 1906)
Morganiae Archaiographia. Rice Merrick 1578 (ed. B. James, South Wales Record Society 1983)
Parochialia. Edward Llwyd (or Lhuyd). Archaeologia Cambrensis supplement 1909-11.

CLASSIFIED LIST OF SITES AND MONUMENTS

In the following list the unnumbered entries relate to additional monuments not mentioned in the text, but which are included here for a more complete record.

Caves (Palaeolithic & later)

(7) Kittle Hill (SS 577 894)
(10) Minchin Hole (SS 555 868)
(11) Bacon Hole (SS 561 868)
(17) Cathole (SS 537 900)
(18) Tooth cave (SS 532 910)
(22) Leather's Hole (SS 530 877)
(39) Longhole (SS 451 850)
(40) Paviland Caves (SS 437 859)
(43) Deborah's Hole (SS 433 863)
(47) Mew Slade caves (SS 423 873)
(50) Worms Head cave (SS 383 877)
(54) Culver Hole (SS 406 939)
(58) Spritsail Tor (SS 426 937)
(63) NorthHill Tor (SS 453 938)
Bosco's Den (SS 559 868)
Crow Hole (SS 558 869)
Caswell Bay cave (SS 589 879)
Cwtch Cave (SS 432 863)
Foresters Cave (SS 551 872)
Port Eynon Point (SS 468 844)
Inner Sound Cave (SS 631 875)
Mumbles hill cave (SS 625 875)
Ravenscliff Cave (SS 547 873)
Rother's Tor Cave (SS 609 874)

Neolithic tombs

(16) Park Cwm (SS 537 898)
(19) Penmaen Burrows (SS 531 882)
(32) Nicholaston long cairn (SS 507 888)
(34) Arthur's Stone (SS 491 905)
(52) Sweyne's Howes (SS 421 898)
(72) Carn Llechart (SS 696 062)

Bronze Age cairns and circles

(34) Great Carn (SS 490 904)
(34) Cefn Bryn (SS 511 891, 503 896)
(34) West of Arthur's Stone (SS 48 90)
(51) Rhossili Down (SS 421 888, 422 893)
(53) Burry Holms (SS 398 926)
(61) Llanmadoc Hill (SS430 927, 440 927)
(68) Pen-y-crug (SS 511 913)
(72) Carn Llechart (SN 698 062)
(71) Carn Goch (SS 605 981)
(74) Carn Llwyd (SN 725 073)
(75) Graig Fawr ring (SN 628 066)
(75) Graig Fawr cairns (SN 623 072, 626 070)
(76) Kilvey Hill (SS 673 939)
(81) Mynydd Drumau (SN 724 004)
(82) Penlle'r Bebyll (SN 635 048)
(85) Tor Clawdd ring (SN 670 063)
Allt-y-grug (SN 751 077)
Banc-john (SN 681 087, 676 083)
Baran Chapel (SN 687 079, 689 075)
Bessie's Meadow (SS 418 900)
Bryn-chwyth (SN 689 081)
Bryn Mawr (SN 690 088)
Carn Twyn (SN 618 027)
Carn Llechart (SN 693 065)
Cefn Bryn groups (SS 492 904, 486 907, 511 891)
Cefn Bryn (east) (SS 520 889)
Cefn Cadle (SS 638 978)
Cefn Gwrhyd (SN 729 078, 731 088, 733 089, 737 096)

Felindre reservoir (SN 655 053)
Hardings Down (SS 438 905)
Mynydd Garn-fach (SN 651 064)
Mynydd Gellionnen (SN 702 046, 703 043)
Mynydd Uchaf (SN 717 101, 719 102, 723 106, 732 110, 735 111)
Mynydd y Garth (SN 708 075, 709 071, 710 077, 713 083)
Newton enclosure (Neolithic henge?) (SS 446 882)
Penhydd-wen (SN 691 071)
Pentre (SN 591 026)
Pen y cwar (SN 633 082)
Pwllfa Watkin group (SN 692 082)
Tir-abbey (SN 727 019)

Bronze Age standing stones

(35) Knelston (SS 468 893)
(35) Burry (SS 464 901)
(66) Sampsons Jack (SS 476 921)
(67) Oldwalls stones (SS 484 919, 487 920)
(74) Cefn Gwrhyd (SN 732 088)
(76) Bon-y-maen (SS 678 952)
(81) Carreg Bica (SS 725 995)
Cefn Celfi (SN 742 031)
Hardings Down (SS 437 908)
Stout Hall (SS 476 891)
Ty'r-coed (SS 437 908)

Iron Age Hillforts and Defended Settlements

(12) High Pennard (SS 568 866)
(13) Bishopston Valley fort (SS 569 878)
(31) Reynoldston (SS 483 899)
(41) Yellowtop (SS 437 860)
(42) Horse Cliff (SS 435 860)
(44) The Knave (SS 431 863)
(45) Thurba Head (SS 422 820)
(46) Lewes Castle (SS 414 873)
(49) Old Castle camp (SS 409 880)
(50) Worms Head fort (SS 393 875)
(53) Burry Holms (SS 400 926)
(56) Hardings Down Forts (SS 435 907)
(61) The Bulwarks (SS 443 927)
(69) Cilifor Top (SS 506 923)
(75) Graig Fawr (SN 618 069)
(76) Kilvey Hill (SS 674 947)
Barland quarry (SS 576 896)
Berry wood (SS 472 885)
Bessie's Meadow (SS 418 901)
Broughton Burrows (SS 408 929)
Brynsifi (SS 483 899)
Carn-nicholas (SS 675 943)
Church Hill (SS 536 898)
Cilonnen (SS 546 938)
Crawley Rocks (SS 519 879)
Druid's Moor (SS 441 901)
Fforest-newydd (SN 636016)
Graig Fawr (SN 622 072)
Grongaer (SS 550 947)
Hen Gastell (SS 554 958)
Henllys (SS 456 887)
Maiden Castle (SS 509 854)
Parkmill (SS 549 892)
Penygaer (SS 536 955)
Redley Cliff (SS 588 875)
Rhossili Down (SS 423 898)
Stembridge (SS 469 914)
Tor-gro (SS 461 935)

Roman sites

(1) Oystermouth 'villa' (SS 616 880)
(71) Carn Goch practice camps (SS 608 972)
(80) Leucarum (Loughor) SS 563 980

Dark Ages sites and inscribed stones

(31) Reynoldston (SS 480 900)
(53) Burry Holms (SS 401 926)
(55) Llangennith (SS 438 914)
(60) Llanmadoc (SS 439 934)
(67) Llanrhidian (SS 496 922)
(78) Llangiwg (SN 724 056)
(79) Llangyfelach (SS 646 990)
(80) Loughor (SS 563 980)
(85) Tor Clawdd dyke (SN 67 06)

Medieval castles and Fortifications

(1) Oystermouth (SS 613 883)
(9) Pennard (SS 544 885)

(21) Castle Tower, Penmaen (SS 534 880)
(27) Norton camp (SS 491 867)
(29) Mountybank, Penrice (SS 492 878)
(30) Penrice castle (SS 497 885)
(63) North Hill Tor (SS 453 938)
(64) Landimore castle (SS 464 932)
(65) Weobley castle (SS 478 927)
(69) Cilifor ringwork (SS 507 922)
(77) Talybont (SN 586 027)
(80) Loughor (SS 564 978)
(83) Penlle'r Castell (SN 665 096)
Barland old castle (SS 583 900)
Cae Castell (SN 694 047)
Leasons wood (SS 488 926)
Swansea New Castle (SS 657 930)

Medieval churches (* ruined sites)

(1) Oystermouth (SS 616 880)
(3) Caswell chapel* (SS 590 883)
(4) Backingstone* (SS 576 881)
(6) Bishopston (SS 578 893)
(8) Pennard (SS 565 887)
(8) Old Pennard* (SS545 885)
(15) Ilston (SS 557 903)
(19) Penmaen* (SS 530 882)
(23) Nicholaston (SS 513 884)
(24) Oxwich (SS 504 861)
(29) Penrice (SS 493 879)
(31) Reynoldston (SS 480 900)
(35) Knelston* (SS 469 890)
(36) Llanddewi (SS 460 890)
(37) Port Eynon (SS 467 854)
(48) Rhossili (SS 416 880)
(48) Old Rhossili* (SS 416 883)
(53) Burry Holms* (SS 401 926)
(55) Llangennith (SS 429 914)
(60) Llanmadoc (SS 439 934)
(62) Cheriton (SS 450 932)
(67) Llanrhidian (SS 497 922)
(70) Llanelen* (SS 511 933)
(77) Llandeilo Talybont* (SN 584 030)
(78) Llangiwg (SN 724 055)
(79) Llangyfelach* (SS 646 990)
Cefn-gorwydd* (SS 588 955)
Cwrt-y-carne* (SN 573 004)
Nicholaston* (SS 523 883)
St Mary's, Swansea (SS 656 929)

Houses and Deserted Medieval Villages

(9) Pennard DMV (SS 545 885)
(19) Penmaen DMV (SS 532 882)
(33) Walterston DMV (SS 509 897)
(48) Rhossili DMV (SS 416 883)
(62) Glebe Farm (SS 451 932)
(73) Cefn Drum DMV (SN 61 04)
(73) Twyn Tyle platform houses (SN 622 047, 624 052)
(75) Graig Fawr platform houses (SN 618 069)
(81) Mynydd Drumau platform houses (SN 727 002, 726 008)
Cross Keys Inn, Swansea (SS 657 929)
Craig y Bedw platform houses (SN 627 042, 628 044)
Cwm Clydach platform houses (SN 672 089)
Nant y Cyrnach long-hut (SN 716 005)
Old Henllys long-hut (SS 449 890)
The Plas (site only) (SS 656 930)

Post-Medieval houses

(2) Nottage farm (site only) SS 605 882
(4) Backingstone (site only) SS 574 881
(5) Great Kittle farm (SS 574 889)
(25) Oxwich Castle (SS 498 863)
(26) Oxwich Green farm (site) SS 496 860
(28) Pitt (SS 493 871)
(36) Llanddewi Castle (SS 460 890)
(57) Delvid (SS 423 928)
(59) Kennexstone (SS 450 916) *now at St Fagans
(62) Cheriton Court (site) SS 451 930
Alltyfanog (SN 696 039)
Alltygraban (SN 604 017)
Alltysgrech (SS 654 960)
Alltygrug (SN 763 094)
Alltwen (SS 578 960)
Barraston (SS 423 909)
Beili-glas (SN 606 038)
Beili-glas (SN 709 111)
Big House (SS 547 897)
Bishopston house (SS 579 889)
Borfa Cottage (SS 468 853)
Box Farm (SS 479 899)
Buan-Llwyd (SN 677 004)
Burry Head (SS 456 903)
Bwthyn (SN 595 038)

Caergynydd (SS 610 950)
Castle Road (SS 612 886)
Cefn Bryn cottage (SS 529 887)
Cefn Eithrim (SN 689 027)
Cefncoed-bach (SS 624 944)
Ceunant (SN 648 070)
Court Farm (SS 463 882)
Courthouse (SS 561 902)
Crwys (SS 574 943)
Cwm-glo (SS 591 942)
Cwm-ivy (SS 439 937)
Cwm-mawr (SS 579 948)
Cwrt-mawr (SN 623 035)
Cynghordy (SN 663 030)
Danybryn (SS 466 854)
Fforest farm (SS 676 983)
Gelli-wern (SN 629 020)
Gerdinen (SN 635 071)
Glan-lliw (SN 613 004)
Glan-y-wern (SS 695 958)
Glynsiling (SS 632 981)
Glyn-y-fid (SN 607 048)
Godre'r-garth (SN 709 065)
Great House (SS 473 859)
Great Pitton (SS 427 875)
Gwenlais-uchaf (SN 618 015)
Henbury (SS 550 880)
Hendre-wen (SN 612 076)
Henllys (SS 448 890)
Heol-las (SS 698 986)
Higher Muzzard (SS 444 914)
Hill's Farm (SS 486 898)
Ivy Cottage (SS 522 883)
Jane's Grove (SS 546 876)
Kilvrough (SS 559 895)
Landimore farm (SS 465 929)
Lanes farm (SS 431 925)
Langrove (SS 565 899)
Little Southgate (SS 550 880)
Llandeilo (SN 584 029)
Llandremor (SN 615 054)
Llanellen (SS 515 934)
Llanmorlais (SS 532 946)
Llangyfelach (SS 654 960)
Llechart-fach (SN 691 048)
Lletygariad (SN 605 039)
Llety Thomas (SN 642 030)
Llwynmeudwy (SN 725 056)
Llwynybwch (SS 484 916)
Llysnini (SS 609 995)
Longoaks (SS 522 892)
Lower Boarspit (SS 605 890)
Maesglwys (SN 654 007)
Meadowside (SS 460 914)
Middle Hills (SS 545 921)
Middleton cottages (SS 422 878)
Neuadd (SN 692 133)
Newton (SS 452 880)
Old Gellihir (SS 563 934)
Overton House (SS 461 854)
Oxwich Cottage (SS 497 866)
Pandy (SN 635 027)
Paviland (SS 445 865)
Pencefnarda (SN 591 024)
Penderi-fawr (SS 619 996)
Penlannau (SN 674 091)
Penllwyn-Robert (SS 538 939)
Penmaen House (SS 527 884)
Penmynydd (SS 438 925)
Pentreprysgedwyn (SN 591 024)
Pentwyn (SN 637 028)
Penyfodau (SS 600 970)
Penypant (SS 647 986)
Penyrallt (SS 492 923)
Pilton Green (SS 445 871)
Pistyll-gwyn (SN 737 082)
Pool House (SS 580 815)
Rhossili farm (SS 416 880)
Rhos-fawr (SN 658 033)
Rose Cottage (SS 465 930)
Rose Cottage (SS 566 881)
Roseland (SS 612 888)
Sanctuary (SS 488 874)
Sketty Green (SS 623 922)
Stormy Castle (SS 446 928)
Stouthall (SS 474 892)
Talyfan (SN 591 050)
Talyffrawe (SS 620 951)
Tanner's Cottage (SS 429 914)
Tile House (SS 462 912)
Tresgyrch (SN 683 090)
Ty Rwsh (SN 598 050)
Upper Hareslade (SS 584 878)
Vine Cottage (SS 466 854)
Waungron (SN 588 021)
West Cathan (SS 434 903)
Wimblewood (SS 552 928)
Windmill farm (SS 477 923)

Ynysforgan (SS 678 990)
Ynystanglwys (SS 686 998)

Miscellaneous Sites

(14) Ilston chapel (SS 553 894)
(19) Pillow mound, Penmaen (SS 534 881)
(29) Penrice old mill (SS 493 882)
(37) The Salt House (SS 469 846)
(38) Culver Hole dovecot (SS 466 845)
(76) Kilvey Hill windmill (SS 674 939)
(84) Scott's Pit enginehouse (SS 696 984)
(84) Gwernllwynchwyth enginehouse (SS 697 980)
(81) Pillow mounds, Mynydd Drumau (SN 726 007)
Earthworks on Carn Goch Common (SS 608 977, 610 975)
Field systems, Rhossili (SS 410 876)
Field systems, Hillend (SS 471 912)
Field systems, Bishopston (SS 585 891)
Shell mounds on Whiteford Burrows (SS 447 956, 442 946)